Mor
Pub Walks in
The Peak District:
The Dark Peak

Les Lumsdon & Martin Smith

Published by Sigma Leisure – an imprint of
Sigma Press, 1 South Oak Lane, Wilmslow, Cheshire SK9 6AR, England.

Whilst every effort has been made to ensure that the information given in this book is correct, neither the publisher nor the author accept any responsibility for any inaccuracy nor for any loss or injury, howsoever caused.

British Library Cataloguing in Publication Data
A CIP record for this book is available from the British Library.

ISBN: 1-85058-298-X

Typesetting and Design by: Sigma Press, Wilmslow, Cheshire.

Maps by: Pam Upchurch

Text photographs: by the authors, except where indicated.

Cover photograph: The Lazy Landlord, Foolow, with the East Cheshire group of the Ramblers Association. Graham Beech

Printed and bound by
Manchester Free Press, Paragon Mill, Jersey St., Manchester M4 6FP.

CONTENTS

The Peak District

Given the outstanding beauty of its landscape, history and culture and its accessibility, it is hardly surprising that the Peak District is so well walked. The Peakland network of paths and tracks is, for the most part, in good order. This is undoubtedly a bonus for those who find their local paths in a far less desirable condition and sometimes obstructed. In contrast the Peak District seems something of a paradise, though there are admittedly still problems.

Peak National Park

There is always likely to be a tension, for the Peak National Park now estimates that there are 22 million visitors each year, the vast majority simply making a day visit for walking or sightseeing or other recreational activity. No one is pretending that this does not bring with it some problems, particularly traffic congestion and parking hassles. Contending with such numbers is not an easy task. That applies to footpaths too, for there can be erosion or other damage. Matters can only improve if we walkers collectively support the conservation work of the various footpath authorities.

One of the great bonuses of enjoying any walk is the ability to adjourn to a local hostelry for a good pint of ale (or other beverage) either at the end of the day or as a respite during the afternoon. Inns have for centuries welcomed the traveller on foot, tradespeople, farmers, miners and quarrymen going to or from their daily work. Now, the country pub is geared to the seeker of leisure, although many still look after a local working population. Despite a shift in clientele, the tradition of hospitality and keeping good beer remains. Here, we take our hats off to The Campaign for Real Ale (CAMRA), which has for the past two decades championed the cause of the real ale drinker and the retention of characterful local pubs. This organisation has done more for the discerning drinker than most big breweries would care to admit.

Tipple

There is a snag, of course, for the rambler who loves real ale. Beer and driving do not mix. All of the rambles in this book feature a pub and several mention two or more *en route*. Those readers who find it impossible to pass a pub without sampling a tipple, should let someone else do the driving. Better still, do as the authors did when researching this volume – use the local bus or train. It helps to keep congestion down and puts money into a vital local facility.

The Dark Peak

This book is a sister publication to 'Pub Walks in The Peak District' which highlighted walks in the White Peak area, the softer limestone areas to be found in the southern realms of the Peak District. Encouraged by the success of this first volume, the authors proceeded to sample the delights of the Dark Peak. This can be defined, roughly speaking, as the northern Peak District plus its western and eastern fringes. The definition has to be loose for this text to avoid duplication with companion books in the series, which includes North Staffordshire, Cheshire and The Pennines.

In 'Pub Walks in The Peak District' the authors speculated on the boundaries of the Peak District, deciding that the territorial limits of the National Park were too restrictive. The same liberal approach applies here. The Peak District is an area of moorland, dale and countryside lying between the conurbations of Manchester and Sheffield, The Potteries and Derby. The emphasis on the Dark Peak takes the walker to the mainly gritstone areas of the Peak, the high northern moors and enchanting hills fringing the western and eastern flanks of the inner limestone plateau. What better sensation than climbing the wilder parts of this high country?

The Peak's Past

The Peak District probably retains more obvious evidence of its past than any other region in England, for it has not been buried in a welter of rebuilding and "improvement". The isolated rugged landscape and harsh climate, particularly on the moorlands, have served to retain ample evidence of the earliest inhabitants and their successors in a way that is remarkable.

The Peakland is the start of the Pennine range of hills, affectionately described by many as "The Backbone of England". The walks featured in this book lie in the first upswellings of these hills, in some of the most spectactular gritsone scenery the Peak has to offer. This is quite unlike the softer limestone character of the central Peak.

Complex Geology

The geology of the area is complex and what follows is obviously a simplification of a process which has spanned millions of years. The Peak is an area of limestone, overlain by gritsones and shales. In the central part of the Peak, the gritsone and shales have largely been eroded away, leaving the limestone exposed. Around the edges and in the north, the gritstones, with their characteristic cloak of dark peat and heather are beloved of the rambler. It was in these environs that the earliest great "battle" for access to the hills was played out, representing a significant triumph for country lovers to gain access into relative wilderness areas.

The Peak District, like most upland areas of Northern Britain, enjoys a moist climate; a typical Derbyshire understatement! The dark peat bogs on Kinder, Bleaklow and Howden Moors are legendary. The rivers are fast flowing and soon attracted the attention of the 18th century industrialist. Few Peakland valleys are wholly lacking evidence of water-powered mills or factories. Similarly, few have escaped the 19th century municipal reservoir. Human endeavour in the landsacpe need not always be detrimental: many of the reservoirs are exceptionally attractive, especially with the backdrop of the hills and trees with which they are so often fringed. Our walks lead to very many of these haunts well known to our antecedents.

Water

Perhaps, the best known of the reservoirs are the three which make up the Derwent Dams complex. The earlier two, Derwent and Howden, are massive stone constructions and are very impressive. These were used for training the Dambuster Squadron during the Second World War. The newest reservoir, Ladybower, is an earth-covered dam, the Peak's biggest single sheet of water. It cradles the two drowned villages of Derwent and Ashopton. Other settlements vanished too because of the need for water by the surrounding cities. In the woodlands around the reservoirs there are the remains of farmsteads, abandoned when the land was acquired by the water committees.

Above the valleys there is a fear of an exodus from the hill farms mainly because of the regulation of farming by the European Community. This will bring a change to the landscape again, for the tide of human encroachment onto the moors has ebbed and flowed throughout the centuries.

Early Settlement

There is abundant evidence of early settlement on the high gritsone moors, dating thousands of years before the Roman Conquest. Village sites, field systems, fortresses, burial places, all are there in areas like Big Moor, east of Baslow, now inhospitable heather and bracken-clad moorland. The earliest known trackways date from these pre Roman times, linking past centres of population and culture together. Some are used in these walks.

The Roman occupation left less impression on the Dark Peak than in the White Peak, but some walks use Roman thoroughfares. One such road headed from Glossop over to Brough and thence to Derby. One came up from Leek to Buxton, then to Brough and over to Rotherham. One ran from Buxton to Glossop via Hayfield, and another from Buxton to Manchester. Remains of all these exist and are still used by the walker. As a measure of the change that has taken place since the legions left, it is worth remembering that the Roman road across the Snake Pass has been covered by six feet of peat, which has grown in the intervening period. The first retreat from the uplands was a combination of climatic and technological change. The weather grew colder and wetter, and technologically the equipment became available to clear the denser woods and to plough the heavier soils of the valleys.

Saxon occupation came late to the Peak District, as evidenced by the survival of Celtic place names like Dinas, Derwent and Eccles. Even the name of the Peak's highest hill, Kinder Scout, is thought to derive from the Celtic *Cwm Dwr Scwd*, meaning 'The Valley of the Waterfall'. This seems an odd name for a hill until you remember Kinder's best-known feature – The Downfall. Later conquerors like the Danes and Normans laid a veneer on the ancient bones of Peakland, adding their castles and settlements. Many of the old names are retained, as in such sprawling Christian parishes as Hope.

In the Norman period, huge tracts of the High Peak became royal hunting forest, subject to the severest of forest laws. Never a true wooded forest, the Peak Forest required wild unpopulated country to be a success. Settlements were forcibly cleared and the inhabitants dispersed to achieve this. The high moors of Kinder and Bleaklow formed the Longdendale ward of the Peak Forest. The Hope and Edale valleys became known as the Hopedale ward, and the area between Buxton and Hayfield, *Campagna*. The boundaries between the wards were marked and Edale Cross is believed to be one such marker.

Certain key officials of the Forest are remembered in pub names like the Woodruffe Arms in Hope: the Woodreeve being responsible for upholding Forest law. Through the centuries the history of the Forest has been concerned with attempts by farmers and others to encroach upon this land.

Faith

In the Middle Ages, sometimes know as the Age of Faith, travel needed a hefty slice of that commodity, especially in the Dark Peak. The lonely wayside crosses such as Edale, Hope and Lady Crosses spring to mind, as markers in the wilderness. There are many others, some still serve that function now, but for the rambler. From these times came the footpad and later the highwayman. The Peak District was a dangerous place for the salter making his way with waggon loads of this precious commodity from the lowlands of Cheshire to the eastern Pennines. The legends of local highwaymen abound, particularly in the western fringes between Buxton and Whaley Bridge.

With the onset of the agrarian and industrial revolutions, the scene again was one of encroachment onto the moors, but at a much faster rate. Enclosure and land improvement were the order of the day, to provide food to feed the nearby fast-growing industrial towns. With this came transport improvement, the widening and straightening of the old packhorse and cart routes. Most of the present main road network dates from the latter half of the 18th century and the first quarter of the 19th. Many older routes have reverted to pleasant grassy tracks, trodden only by the occasional pedestrian.

Jenkin Chapel, up in the hills near Windgather Rocks and located on an old salter's trail extending from Northwich to Yorkshire

As pressure for cultivation mounted, more land was taken into farming, a process aided by improved machinery, climate and the increased grazing of sheep. Catastrophies brought about by the deepest of economic troughs eventually led to the abandonment of these marginal lands or their conversion to vast sheep walks. At this time too, there was almost a reversion to the old Forest laws, with attempts by landowners to close off access to the high moors and even to stop off ancient rights of way. This was all in the interests of sheep farming and the breeding of grouse.

The early debates focused on the need to manage moorlands, the disruptive effect of walkers, the "right" to roam open moorlands and so on. The National Park movement in this country was, largely, fuelled by this debate. High profile events such as mass trespasses and the battles for Kinder are still celebrated each year. Walkers using this book will come across both access land, where they can wander at will and private moor, where the only access is the public right of way crossing it.

For some, the name "Dark Peak" sounds uninviting. It is, admittedly, a harsher environment than the White Peak, but there are compensations, its wildness, dramatic scenery, the interplay of rocks, heather and cascading water. Do not take our word for it. Don your boots now and make for the Peak District's highest hills.

The Walks

The walks vary in length from four to ten miles and in terms of exertion required. The Chinley walk, for example, is easy going, but the Ashopton or Hope rambles include many more climbs and some rough terrain. There are thirty rambles to choose from and before embarking on one there are a few golden rules.

Do not trust the weather. Always go prepared with a waterproof and a warm woollen. It might well be sunny when walking in the valley below, but on the high moorlands the wind chill, even in summer, can be discomforting. In Winter it can be dangerous. The weather can turn wild, so please be prepared. It is easy enough to take a light rucksack with the waterproofs and a light snack in case the walk takes longer than you first imagined.

The walks should be easy to follow by simply using a good map and the instructions in the book. There tend to be two main problems regarding instructions for the reader. The first relates to how the authors perceive the route and describe it. They might consider a green lane to be the main feature and write this up accordingly. You might only see the tractor tracks and therefore miss the intended route. If you do find yourself off the prescribed route, retrace your steps to a point where you found the text to be absolutely clear and then look again at the points mentioned by the authors to aid navigation. We quite expect you to curse us more than once!

The second point relates to when things change. As the countryside is a working environment, field patterns, areas of woodland and buildings change. Please accept our apologies in advance for this. The text has been written so that even if a hedge is grubbed up or a woodland felled, the way should still be easy to follow, despite the loss of an occasional landmark.

The Pubs

Publicans in the Peak District usually welcome ramblers and all of those in this book have been approached by the authors to ensure that details of opening times and the like are accurate at the time of writing

Most country pubs in the land have changed in the past two to three decades to survive. The first major change is that most pubs serve food. This has become so important to their trading pattern that publicans only allow people, ramblers or otherwise, to eat food bought on their premises. Most of the pubs in this book offer bar meals at lunch and in the evening but not usually the entire session – more likely noon to 2 pm and 7 pm until 9 to 9.30 pm. Unless stated in the text the pub concerned does not allow eating your own food on the premises.

The same applies to muddy boots. Witness the increasing numbers of hastily-written notes on pub doors: " Hikers Welcome . . . Remove Your Boots!" Most pubs now have no bar with stone flagged or wooden floors where boots and wellies are accepted. Most rooms tend to be carpeted. Thus, it makes sense to kick off your boots before entering to avoid the offence of being asked to do this. In some instances, pubs have boot racks and storage areas in the porch for rucksacks. Cunning ramblers will take a pair of clean overshoes and avoid the hassle of boot removal.

The question of families in pubs often arises. Every publican in the book is happy to welcome families, especially if children are well behaved. Most have gardens or outdoor seats for summer use and this is ideal for the family group. Children are also welcome indoors if there is a separate area or room away from the bar. This the law. So, it makes sense for mum or dad to simply pop a head around the door to ask whether it is all right bring in the family! Both authors have families and have not found difficulties at lunch or early evening. Some hostelries feel they are not geared up for families at all times of the week and say so, such as The Leather's Smithy on the Tegg's Nose ramble.

The fortunate point is that many of the Peak District pubs have not moved completely into the restaurant business, but offer a warm friendly place to stop awhile and refresh oneself after a thirsty mile or two. The pubs are steeped in history and often reflect the locality they were built to serve. Long may they survive.

The authors endorse wholeheartedly the 'Countrygoer' concept, a campaign to encourage countryside lovers to leave their car at home whenever there is a bus or train alternative. This can add to the fun of the day and many of the walks included are accessible by public transport every day of the week – Sundays too!

Derbyshire County Council produces a superb timetable booklet detailing all services in The Peak District and offers a BUSLINE telephone service for would-be travellers. The current telephone numbers are:

Derby (0332) 292200; Buxton (0298)23098; Chesterfield (0246) 250450

Some rail information is available on the same numbers, but ring BR for more detailed and current train times and fares.

However you decide to travel, the authors hope that you have as much fun walking these routes as they had researching them. The Peak District is a rambler's paradise. Look after it.

LOCATION MAP

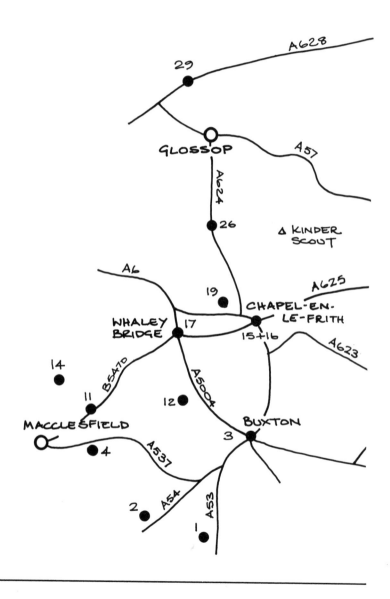

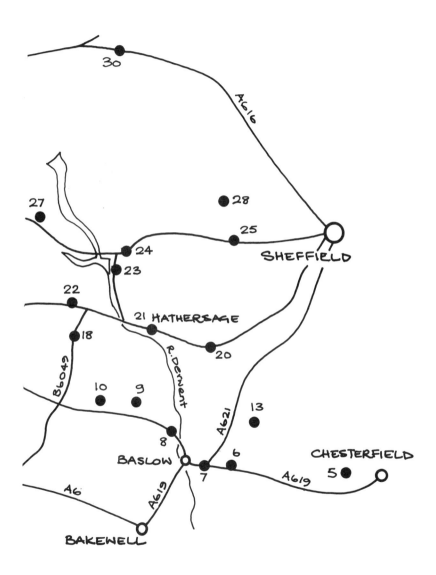

Walk 1: Flash Bar

The Route: Oxensitch, Readyleach Green, Knotbury Common, Three Shire Heads, Hawk's Nest, Flash

Distance: 8 km (5 mls)

Start: The Travellers Rest, Flash Bar (Grid Reference 033677)

Map: Ordnance Survey Outdoor Leisure 24 – The Peak District, White Peak Area

How to get there:

By Bus – There is a daily bus (X23) between Sheffield and The Potteries, supplemented by Bakers' 223 on Sundays.

By Car – Travel on the A53 between Leek and Buxton to Flash Bar. There is a small area for parking near to the pub and stores.

Three Shire Heads has been the subject of many walking books. It is such an intriguing location, quiet now but two hundred years ago a busy junction where bartering, cock fighting and open air boxing took place. It was notorious for villains and the like. This romantic meeting point of three counties, has witnessed many gatherings dispersed by local police.

The Traveller's Rest

The Traveller's Rest stands just off the main Leek to Buxton road, the route used by the Romans. The pub stands on high open ground, 1540 feet (470m) above sea level to be precise, close to the source of the Manifold River. It is not a place to be when the wind is howling. It was probably a pub-cum-farmstead in earlier times which served the traveller between Peak District towns – what a respite it would have been in those early times before the car.

While not serving real ale, this pub offers a warm welcome to the rambler and bottled Guinness is on sale for the purist! The moon-shaped bar is the focal point of the pub, but there is a cosy nook near the fire beneath a splendid picture of an old regular who cycles up from nearby Flash every day. From the rear windows the view down into Upper

Dovedale is magnificent with the unusual shapes of Chrome and Parkhouse hills observed from a different vantage point.

The Travellers Rest is open from 11 am until 3 pm and from 6 pm on an evening Monday to Saturday. Usual Sunday hours. Food is served during opening hours except Sunday evening. Next door is The Flash Bar Stores, an epitome of rural enterprise – for the shopper can purchase everything from groceries to electrical goods in this well-loved Moorland institution.

The Walk

Leave The Traveller's Rest and pass by The Flash Bar Stores to the main road. Cross over and turn right to walk by the bus shelter and then turn left along a road signposted to Knotbury. There are exceptional views across the Peak Park and down to the Roaches from here. Pass by Oxensitch at a road junction where a sign warns 'Beware of the Geese!" – they hiss and group themselves in defence until after the rambler is well past. The road continues to descend. At the next junction bear right.

This short stretch of road leads to a farm at Readyleach Green. At the junction go left through a gate to enter a field strewn with bits of old cars and machinery. It is a shame that so much debris surrounds the many farmsteads in this area. Farming has never been sufficient on its own, so many supplemented their income by being pedlars or working in local quarries or mines. In more recent times, repair work, scrap metal and road haulage have provided some local employment. Keep ahead to cross a broken wall and on to cross a ladder stile, with yet another dumped car.

Knotbury Common

Turn right along a track to Knotbury Common. The track begins to descend, passes barns and a cottage on the left before falling more steeply into the valley. The path leads over a tractor bridge to join another track. Go left and through a gate. The track forks and you keep left by the cascading brook as it cuts its way down to Panniers Pool. This is an old name referring to its use by packhorse trains in earlier centuries. Another track joins from the left and the old "road" drops down to Three Shires Bridge – the meeting place of Cheshire, Derbyshire and Staffordshire.

Dane Valley

Before the bridge, go left along a sandy route. At the next gate, keep to the higher track along the edge of the Dane Valley, which can be seen rolling away towards Cheshire. The track becomes more made up and

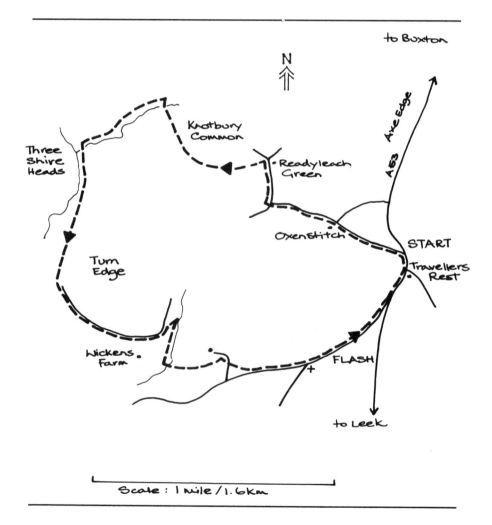

Scale : 1 mile / 1.6 km

curves left by an old farmstead where you may note the outside toilet (private, of course). The road now becomes metalled and continues through a gate, curving left to climb another clough.

Beneath the cottage look for a path bearing right back down the clough. It is well worn and leads down to a wicket gate. Once through, proceed down to a four-directional signpost supplied by The Peak and Northern Footpath Society, which has done so much to keep our rights of ways open.

Brace yourself, for the next mile or so is a steep climb to Flash. Go left, crossing the bridge to climb to a stile. Look back to Wickens Farm, where the remains of a railway guard's van can look ghostly on a misty morning. Once across, climb up the bank through scrub and gorse towards a dry stone wall on the right. Cross a stile and keep ahead to another, the dry stone wall being to your right. Keep ahead in the next field, and soon a stile by a small gate can be seen. Cross this and proceed to a wooden stile leading onto a drive.

Flash

Go right for approximately a hundred paces, then left through a gap in the fence. Head slightly right up the field to a stile, with great views back down the Dane valley. Go through the very narrow enclosure to exit onto a road. Turn left and walk the short distance into Flash, at one time the centre of counterfeiting and robbery. Hence the term "flashy" meaning something that looks good but might not be all it seems. The villainy hereabouts became so rife that a crack force of police was despatched from Chester to finally rout the robbers. Since then, the locals have settled down to more peaceful pastimes. On the left is the old Wesleyan chapel dating from 1784 and on the right, past the pub, a stone commemorating the opening of the school in 1760. The church stands windswept at the head of the community.

Continue ahead to pass the new school and proceed to the main road. Bear left and cross the road to walk along a wide verge to The Travellers Rest.

Walk 2: Wildboarclough

The Route: Higher Nabbs, Lower Nabbs Farm, Owlers Bridge, Rose and Crown – Allgreave, Clough Brook

Distance: 7 km (4 mls)

Start: Lay-by at Brookside, near The Crag Inn (Grid Reference 981682)

Map: Ordnance Survey Outdoor Leisure 24 – The Peak District, White Peak Area

How to get there:

By Bus – There is a limited bus service from Macclesfield, including Sunday mornings throughout the year

By Car – Travel on the A54 and then A537 from Buxton. Wildboarclough is signposted off this route. From Macclesfield travel on the A537 road. Turn right at Anchor Lane and right at The Stanley Arms for Wildboarclough. There is a lay-by just beyond The Crag Inn.

Standing on its own beneath Allgreave Hill, the Rose and Crown is a stubborn survivor. It was built as a wayside inn and smithy and has beckoned many a weary traveller on a cold winter's night. It serviced the Congleton to Buxton toll road in the early part of the last century. There are two rooms, both offering views out into the valley below, with tables set back from the bar. The pub is used to cyclists and walkers popping in. The beer garden is behind the house.

The pub is open noon to 3 pm on Mondays to Saturdays and from 7 pm in the evenings. Usual Sunday hours. Bar meals are available on Wednesdays through to Mondays, there being sandwiches only on offer on Tuesdays. Robinsons Best Bitter and, in winter, Old Tom are on draught. The latter should be treated with caution as it is a winter brew which has a nasty habit of altering the vision if taken in large measures.

The Walk

The walk starts from the lay-by alongside Clough Brook at Brookside, not far beyond The Crag Inn, featured in Sigma Leisure's "Pub Walks in

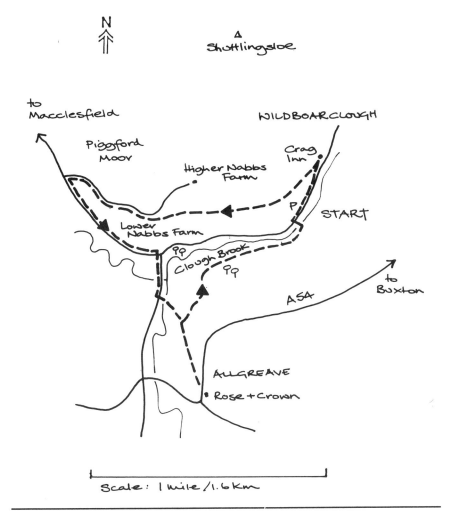

N

Shuttlingsloe

to Macclesfield

WILDBOARCLOUGH

Piggford Moor

Higher Nabbs Farm

Crag Inn

P   START

Lower Nabbs Farm

Clough Brook

to Buxton

A54

ALLGREAVE

Rose + Crown

Scale: 1 mile / 1.6 Km

Cheshire". Wildboarclough is an intriguing place. No more than a dispersed hamlet now, it was a thriving mill centre until the early 1950s, with cottages named after some of the workers' home cities such as Edinburgh and Glasgow. Walk back to the car park entrance of The Crag Inn where there is a charming notice asking people to slow down because of the ducks crossing. There is a step-stile on the left. Cross this and climb up the hillside slightly right between hawthorn bushes. Just beyond these trees, the path curves more sharply right to a stone step-stile, where there is a less-than-charming notice advising walkers to keep to the path.

Higher Nabbs

Keep ahead in the next field to the ladder stile ahead after a dip and stream. The line of the route is clearly marked by the stiles ahead. Go straight on again to cross a stone step-stile next and then bear right to another ladder stile. Higher Nabbs Farm stands to the right across the field. Keep ahead with an old wall to your left and cross the next ladder stile. Pass just to the right of a group of boulders. Then, bear slightly right to cross a gully and turn left towards a stile next to a gate. Go over it and keep ahead to a gateway near to a dry stone wall. Go left on the track, through a stile and then climb away from the track to a stile on the right which exits onto a metalled farm access road.

Turn left and follow the road up the valley edge below Piggford Moor. At the junction with the next metalled road, bear left to pass through Lower Nabbs farm which offers horse riding. Note the stone dog kennel on the left. The road descends to a junction by a bungalow. Go right and very shortly look for a path on the right leading to Owlers Bridge which spans the brook.

It is hard to imagine that, a few years ago, this was a raging torrent which swept footbridges away and damaged houses and barns near to its banks.

Rose and Crown

Once over the bridge go right, along the water's edge and then follow the old track as it climbs away by a wood to a junction. Keep ahead for the last section to the main road and Rose and Crown public house. Sometimes, the section along the river becomes flooded or extremely wet. If this is the case, use the footpath from the bridge which keeps ahead to cross a stile. It then continues up a field boundary to the right of a barn and exits by way of a stile onto a green lane. Those going to the pub should turn right here and follow it to a gate and then onto the Rose and Crown as described above. Walkers not seeking refreshment can turn left at the old barn.

Assuming you have been to the pub, retrace your steps to the junction of tracks. Take the higher way by crossing a stile by a gate. The green track passes the barn and skirts a wood, often busy with noisy rooks, before coming to a cottage and barn. Keep ahead beyond the cottage, keeping company with the dry stone wall on the left. The track leads through a gap in a wall. After this, your way is to drop down towards the brook. Remain on the higher level of the bank rather than closer to the water's edge.

Cross a stile and walk straight on to another. Then walk a little further to the drive of the Brookside restaurant. Turn left to cross the brook and then back into Wildboarclough, which now happens to produce gallons of sparkling table water of the same name.

The Brookside Restaurant, Wildboarclough; The Crag Inn
is just a stroll away

Walk 3: Buxton

The Route: Burbage, Berry Clough, Goyt's Clough, Deep Clough, Stake Clough, Cat and Fiddle, Derbyshire Bridge, Macclesfield Old Road

Distance: 16 km (10 mls)

Start: Buxton Railway station (Grid Reference 058777) or Burbage Church (Grid Reference 044728)

Map: Ordnance Survey Leisure 24 – The Peak District, White Peak Area

How to get there:

By Bus and Train – Buxton has a daily bus and train service from Manchester. It is also well served by buses from Derby, Sheffield, The Potteries and at weekends from Macclesfield

By Car – Travel to Buxton then on the A53 road to Burbage church traffic lights where you turn right into Macclesfield Old Road. This is residential, so please park considerately.

No specific pub is chosen for this walk. The route passes by the Cat and Fiddle where there is a functional walkers' bar. There are also several interesting pubs in or near The Market Place in Buxton. The authors recommend The Cheshire Cheese which sells fine Kimberley ales, The Old Sun with Marston's beers and the New Inn serving Robinsons beers – including the rare dark mild. Between them they offer service for most of the day.

Those travelling to Buxton by rail should turn right outside the station and at the roundabout pass the gardens of The Palace Hotel. Cross the road by the junction and walk up St John's Road for about a mile to Burbage church. Bus travellers arriving at The Market Place should walk to the left of the town hall down to the Pavilion Gardens and pass The Opera House to join St John's Road. Bear left and continue to Burbage church where you turn right into Macclesfield Old Road. An easier option is to take the 198 bus to its Burbage terminus, Level Lane. This is adjacent to Macclesfield Old Road.

Pavilion Gardens, Buxton

The Walk

Walk up Macclesfield Old Road and eventually leave houses to pass over the old track bed of the Cromford and High Peak Railway. Soon afterwards look for a stile on the right leading into woodland. Cross it and bear left up to a corner. Take the right fork across the rough ground, easing away from the dry stone wall on the right. This well-used path leads diagonally across this large field curving first right, then left up to a stile in the top far-right corner.

Berry Clough

This leads onto high moorland with a breeze at any time of year. Continue ahead to meet another path coming in from the left. The path descends to a stream in Berry Clough and continues to drop down to a bridge and then up to a road.

Go left here into Goyt's Clough. At a niche on the right, go right as

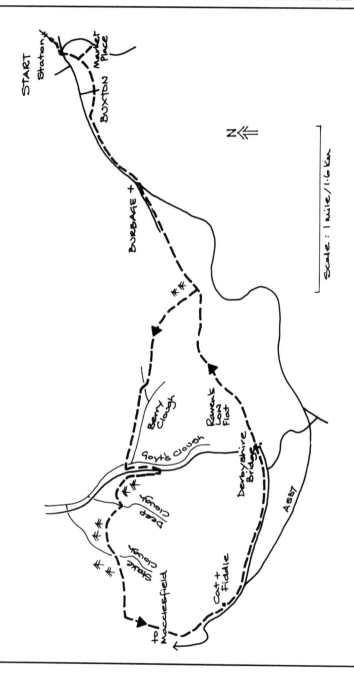

signposted along a track which runs beside a wood and soon leads into it by way of a stile.

Remorseless Climb

The path climbs through the wood, clear enough but very wet in winter. It drops down to a stream in Deep Clough and then climbs again to eventually reach a ladder stile. Surmount the stile and go right here, following the perimeter fence around to Stake Clough which is not incised at this point. Follow the clear waymarked path as it curves right and leaves the wood behind to climb remorselessly out of the valley. Keep close to the dry stone wall on the right and eventually, after sweat and toil, reach a wall and track on higher ground.

Turnpike Road

Your way lies to the left along the track, above a farm and roadside restaurant. Meet another track coming in from the left and follow this left towards the main road. This is the old turnpike road dating back to 1759. Look for the old milestone on the left showing the mileage to London! There is also the inscription 'J. Thurman 1892'. One wonders what he was doing at the time.

At the main road, which is the 1823 turnpike, walk along the verge to the Cat and Fiddle Inn, dating from the 1830s when it was financed by a Macclesfield banker with spare cash. It is very popular in summer, but can get snowed in during the winter. Walk past the pub and turn left at the next junction following the lane down to Derbyshire Bridge. Keep ahead by the Visitor Centre and follow the old turnpike road once again as it climbs up Raven's Low. It then descends to Burbage, the last section offering easy walking after a number of strenuous climbs.

Buxton

Most people think of Buxton as being in the hills. It is, but from this vantage point it can be seen to be sheltering in a valley. Loved by the Romans, Buxton has managed to retain and redevelop itself as a resort. The Crescent and the Devonshire Hospital are masterpieces which need careful conservation. The Pavilion Gardens and Opera House are equally priceless and have adapted well to modern needs. Buxton is becoming increasingly attractive to the short stay and day visitor.

Walk 4: *Tegg's Nose*

The Route: Walker Barn, Ashtreetop, Macclesfield Forest, Leather's Smithy, Bottoms Reservoir, Teggs Nose Country Park

Distance: 8 km (5 mls)

Start: Tegg's Nose Country Park. (Grid Reference 951733).

Map: Ordnance Survey Outdoor Leisure 24 – The Peak District, White Peak Area

How to get there:

By Bus – There is a weekend bus service to Tegg's Nose Country Park

By Car – Travel on the A537 between Buxton and Macclesfield. The country park is signposted from this road.

It is said that the Leather's Smithy pub was in earlier times known as the New Inn. It stands alongside a packhorse route through Macclesfield Forest. In the last century a blacksmith by the name of William Leather took the place on and ran it as a smithy and a pub of the same name. The blacksmith's trade has long since gone, but the pub remains to quench the thirst of the rambler.

The pub has three rooms: a lounge, a small back room and a bar with stone-flagged floor and open fire. This back room is often used by families, who are welcome at weekend lunchtimes only, and at other times in the garden to the rear. Food is served at lunchtimes and evenings but not throughout the sessions, which are 11 am until 3 pm Monday to Saturday, and from 7 pm in the evening. Usual Sunday opening.

Tetley Mild and Bitter, Jennings Bitter and Snecklifter are on draught and kept in excellent condition. The pub gets very busy on a summer weekend given its location. It is always well-patronised by walkers and local people. It is not unusual to see dogs, horses and rucksacks outside waiting to be collected by their errant owners!

Walking in the Country Park (Courtesy of Chris Rushton)

The Walk

Start from the Visitor centre at Tegg's Nose Country Park. Turn right to leave the country park and walk, facing the traffic, up the road past Windyway House. Traffic travels too fast for this road, so be wary of oncoming vehicles. Go down the hill to pass a chapel and to the junction at the main road opposite The Setter Dog. This is a splendid pub (serving Marstons) which always gives a welcome to the walker and is featured in 'Pub Walks in Cheshire', also published by Sigma.

Crooked Yard Farm

Turn right for a few paces along the main road and turn right along a minor road signposted to Crooked Yard Farm. Pass Lower Windyway Farm and look for a ladder stile on the left. Go over this and follow the path as it bears right up the hillside. Climb over a stone water trough and then gain ground to another ladder stile which is crossed, not without difficulty, for it is of mammoth proportions.

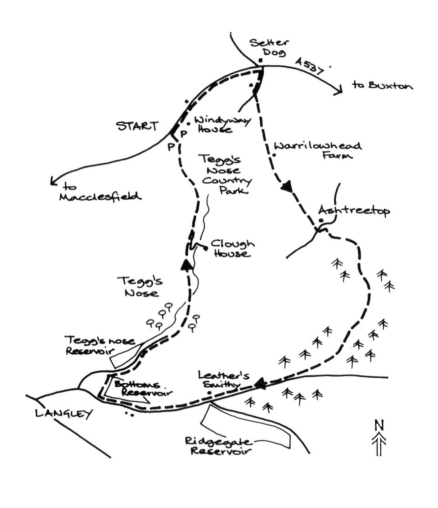

Scale: 1 mile /1.6Km

The views across to Tegg's Nose and into the Bollin valley below are marvellous. Make your way up to the access track to Warrilowhead Farm. Go right along it, but at the gateway cross the stile to the right. The path continues ahead below the renovated farmhouse. Pass through the gap where there are several magnificent stone troughs and a cast iron bath. Keep ahead to cross a stile in a field corner, then follow the path as it curves slightly left. Move a little away from the dry stone wall, and admire the views across to Macclesfield Forest.

The path descends the first of two cloughs, steepening as it cuts through gorse and scrub down to a stream. It climbs again to come alongside a low level dry stone wall. Continue ahead to descend the second clough. Look for a way through the wet ground, then ensure that you rise out of the dip to walk ahead with the dry stone wall to the left.

As you approach Ashtreetop you soon cross a stile. There has been a recent diversion here, so the map is slightly inaccurate. Your way is now ahead through a small plantation with the buildings to your left. Enter the lane by way of the next stile. Bear left and then right into the wood.

Macclesfield Forest

The woodland walk leads to a junction with another track. Bear left and follow this wider way up to an old barn known as Dimples. There is a meeting of tracks here. Take the lower track by the barn, then at the next junction bear right to continue along a main route through Macclesfield Forest. This area was once part of a Royal hunting forest, referring to a territory which was once the subject of the strictest of laws. The present woodland belongs to North West Water plc, and the predominant species are pine, spruce and larch.

The track eventually leads down to a metalled road which links Langley with Forest Chapel, an isolated hamlet with a picturesque chapel where a rush-bearing ceremony is held annually. Turn right and follow the road to the Leather's Smithy where a road comes in from the left. There are good views across Ridgegate Reservoir.

Bottoms

Continue down the road and soon you come to Bottoms Reservoir on your right. This was built in 1850 with a maximum depth of 32 feet and a capacity of 34 million gallons to serve nearby Macclesfield. There are cottages to the left and not far along there is a stile on the right allowing access onto the bank of the reservoir. Follow the path, which is on the Gritstone Trail, a regional walking route between Rushton Spencer and Lyme Park. Go along the edge of the reservoir and then right and up across the dam to climb steps over a sluice to a track.

Turn right here for the return to Tegg's Nose, although a harder route is waymarked ahead. On the left is Tegg's Nose Reservoir which was built in 1871 and has a maximum depth of 37 feet but with a smaller capacity than Bottoms. The route climbs gently alongside the country park with the infant River Bollin to the left and soon to be crossed. The track leads through a pasture with a little pond to the right and wooden bench to the left. Look for a track just beyond leading off left down to stepping stones over the river.

Climb up the path to the stile on the left and, once over, bear right. You stand beneath the gritstone outcrops which were quarried until the 1950s. An outdoor exhibition in the higher reaches of the park tells the story of rock extraction, and how gritstone was quarried, cut and prepared for local use.

Saddler's Way

The path leads right to a stile by a gate and onto a track above Clough House. This soon joins a metalled road. Go left and at the next corner keep ahead along a bridleway known as Saddlers Way which climbs remorselessly back to the car park at the Visitor Centre. On the right here is the viewfinder which allows the walker to spot the route just followed. There is the haunting shape of Shutslingsloe in the back-ground. Alternatively make a bee-line to the refreshment kiosk to sink a cup of tea or lick an ice cream as a reward for the last climb.

Walk 5: Old Brampton

The Route: Ashgate Hospice, Broomhall Farm, Frith Hall, Bagthorpe Farm, Riddings, Wigley, Birley Brook, Linacre Reservoir, Woodnook

Distance: 9 km (6 mls)

Start: Ashgate Hospice. (Grid Reference 348716).

Map: Pathfinder Sheet 761 – Chesterfield

How to get there:

By Bus – There is a daily service from Chesterfield which stops at the hospice.

By Car – Travel on the A619 from Chesterfield, turn right along Old Road signposted to Old Brampton. From the west, travel on the A619 past the Terminus Hotel, then first left onto the B6150, and left at the next crossroads signposted to Old Brampton. There is limited parking on the roadside just beyond the Hospice.

The Royal Oak near Wigley, which was to an earlier generation of drinkers as "Florrie's Place" after a former landlady, is as welcoming as ever. The Royal Oak is open from 11.30 am until 3.30 pm and from 6.30 pm on Mondays to Saturdays. Usual Sunday hours. Tetleys draught bitter is on offer and food is served. There is a patio area for summer drinking.

The Walk

From the bus stop by the Hospice, walk up the road towards Old Brampton and at the right hand bend, go left down the signposted public bridleway. At the fork in the lane go right. The rough lane is fenced and hedged throughout as it dips gently to cross a stream before rising again to Broomhall Farm, an unusually tall thin red brick building. At a T-junction, just beyond the farm, go straight on into a hollow way.

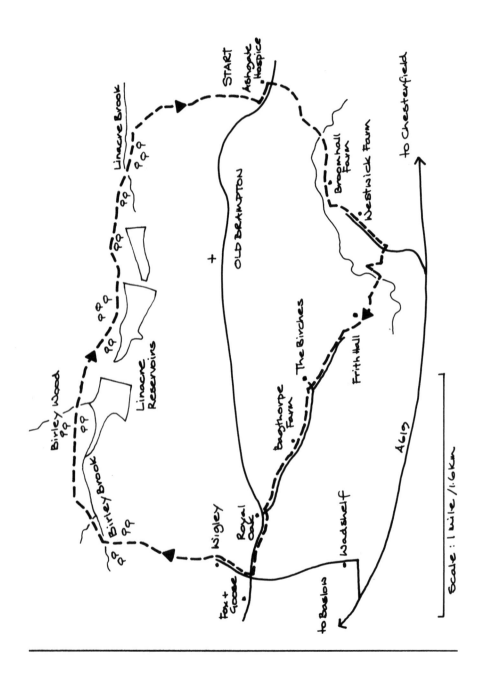

Frith Hall

At Westwick Farm, there is a view across to Old Brampton church and the lane now becomes metalled. At the bungalow, go right and descend steeply to Wood Farm. At the farm, the track goes sharp left and crosses the stream again. It then rises between holly hedges, eventually reaching Frith Hall. The hall dates from 1804 but the name Frith is Norman, meaning forest. Its most common occurrence in the Peak District is in and around the town, Chapel-en-le-Frith.

A stile by a gate carries the walker out of the yard of Frith Hall onto a lane again. Note the fine chicken coop on the right!

Follow the lane to The Birches and bear left. The view here stretches across to Stone Edge with its lead smelt chimney and to Bole Hill at Wingerworth. The ever present plume of steam and smoke comes from Avenue Carbonisation plant south of Chesterfield. Wadshelf village forms the western horizon, while eastwards the sun catches the limestone walls of Bolsover Castle. Continue along the lane. Beyond the gate at Bagthorpe Farm the lane becomes metalled up to the main road opposite the Royal Oak. Bear left here, following the main road. There is a footway on the left hand side, which is fortunate because motorists do have a tendency to come down the hill at quite a pace.

Walk to the cross roads at Wigley. Wigley school is ahead and on the left, with the Fox and Goose pub opposite. Go right at the crossroads, glancing back down the valley to Chesterfield and beyond. Ignore the left turn to Moorhay Farm, bearing right along the lane. There is a surprising view from here, as cars can be seen almost on the horizon at Owler Bar.

Wigley

The lane swings left into the metropolis of Wigley. Go between the buildings. Where the track swings right into Wigley Hall Farm, continue ahead (i.e. not left) through a stile (which is signposted), taking care to avoid a well-hidden ditch. From this point you can see Cutthorpe and Sheffield ahead, but these rapidly disappear as the walker descends a walled track, paved in part with "Causey stones". These are usually a sure guide of an ancient and well used track. This one is fringed with trees, elms and sloes. At the fork, go left. The right-hand path vanishes and is not shown on the map. Continue to descend through an oak wood to a stream.

Cross the stream, and then fork right to cross another stream by a bridge. A stile and bridge take you over another stream and into open fields. Go right here by the Birley Brook. This is not as shown on the Ordnance Survey map but is the route walked by locals nevertheless. The path is not always distinct, but keeps the stream on the right, crossing a tributary brook near an oak tree by stepping stones. Just beyond the brook a path climbs left up the bank. Ignore this and proceed along by the main stream, crossing a ditch until brought up short by a wall and barbed wire entanglement. A waymark points you alongside the wall and through an encroaching thicket of hawthorn. There's a stile on the right which leads into Birley Woods.

Linacre Reservoirs

Here at last the path becomes distinct again, winding its way through the trees. Ignore the bridge, glimpsed below on the right and keep on narrow upper path, which soon forks left and runs along quite a distinct terrace. The first of the series of reservoirs can be seen below and also a wide path. Ignore this until your path descends quite steeply to join the track at a culvert and bridge. Go left and walk along the lakeside path to the top dam. The path goes down to the dam wall then bears left. Beyond the top dam the track is wide with occasional glimpses down to the middle reservoir. The path comes alongside the second lake and there are picnic tables and seats for those needing a rest. Continue straight on along a wide path, past the middle dam, bearing right at the T-junction. Go through the gate, then right again on the lane. The third and lowest dam is now in view. These dams were built to serve the burgeoning town of Chesterfield and are known as Linacre reservoirs.

Do not descend to the dam unless you need to patronise the loo, but carry on, forking right by the lamp post along a rough track. This soon descends to cross the Linacre Brook and reaches a junction of paths. Do not go over the footbridge to the left, but continue ahead keeping the stream on your left.

Holme Hall

The track soon leaves the stream and rises out of the wood to be greeted by the vanguard of the housing sprawl of Chesterfield. This is Holme Hall estate, a further example of Chesterfield's lopsided development which encroaches on the fringes of the Peak, swallowing old hamlets in the process. Will it sprawl to where you stand now?

With the crooked spire of Chesterfield church visible over the rooftops continue by Woodnook Cottage, and reach the road just west of the hospice. Turn left to reach the bus stop and car parking area.

Walk 6: Robin Hood

The Route: Robin Hood, Gardom's Edge, Jack Flat, Wellington's Monument, Eagle Stone, Clod Hall Cross Roads, Nelson's Monument, Birchens Edge, Robin Hood

Distance: 7 km (4 mls)

Start: Robin Hood public house (Grid Reference 280721)

Map: Ordnance Survey Leisure No 24 – The Peak District, White Peak Area

How to get there:

By Bus – There is a daily service from Chesterfield, Bakewell, and Manchester

By Car – A619 from Chesterfield at Baslow. Car park signed from the main road.

The Robin Hood is a pub well-known among the rambling and climbing fraternity, nestling as it does at the foot of Birchen's Edge. It sits on the old road, which is fortunate – as the thirsty rambler can sit outside without suffering the bustle of the A619. The Robin Hood is open from 1130 am during the summer months on Mondays to Saturdays and all day on Saturdays only during the winter. On Mondays to Fridays in the winter, opening times are from 11.30 am until 3.30 pm and from 6.30 pm in the evening. Usual Sunday hours.

Serving a cracking pint of Riding Mild, Mansfield Bitter and Old Baily as well as bar food and Sunday lunches, (sandwiches at other times), the Robin Hood is ideal for the walker and is justifiably popular. When entering, note the name of Mr Ollivant on the lintel above the left-hand entrance. An extract from "This Week" dated 20 July 1889 tells an amusing tale:

"At Bakewell on Saturday, before Mr R.W.M. Nesfield, Catherine Stevenson, of Nottingham, in custody, was charged with breaking several panes of glass in the window of The Robin Hood public house near Baslow, on the previous night.

A man, said to be her husband, tried to prevent Mr Ollivant the
landlord, from securing the woman. With assistance, he put both into an
outbuilding and kept them there until the police arrived. Both were then
conveyed to the Bakewell Lock-up. The woman had torn one of the legs
off the man's trousers whilst in the outbuilding. He was discharged and
the woman sent to prison for fourteen days."

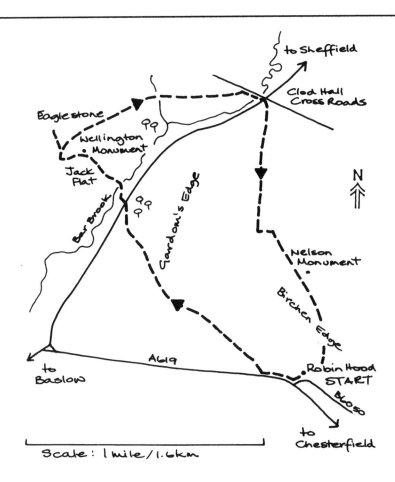

Scale: 1 mile/1.6km

The Walk

Leave the Robin Hood public house and go right, down to the road junction. Follow the main A619 road towards Baslow for a short distance until you reach a stile and signpost on the right. Go over this and into fields. The path crosses a terrace, the line of the old Chesterfield road which was turnpiked in 1758. It was superseded by the present A619 road in the late eighteenth century and a toll house was erected at Robin Hood.

The path climbs up onto rough pasture land and according to the map passes through a series of ancient enclosures. It takes a well-trained eye to spot these, though these eastern moors were settled in the Bronze Age. The inhabitants have left a wealth of artefacts for the historian to discover.

As the path tops the rise, there is a view on the right to Birchen's Edge and the Nelson Monument. To the left, the land plunges steeply to the Barbrook with a view into the central Peak, to Eaglestone Flat and the Wellington Monument.

Continue on the main path (rather than a narrow path heading off to the right along the wall), and descend the steep slopes below Gardoms Edge, soon becoming embroiled in scrubby birch woodland. Nevertheless, it is an easy and pleasant walk, dropping steadily down to a stile which takes you out onto the main A621 road.

The Wellington Monument

Beware of the stile for it is perilously close to a watertrough. There is also little or no verge on this side of the road. Cross the road with care and descend the path opposite down to Barbrook, which you cross. The path begins to climb to the Wellington monument. A steep direct assault, first in fields and then through woodland up what is known in best Derbyshire tradition of understatement as Jack Flat. But there again, all things are relative.

Nearing the monument, the path veers left, still climbing, beneath the rocky outcrop on which the column is based. There are various direct lines of ascent, but it is easier to keep along the clear path and then back along the top of the rocks. The monument was built to commemorate

Wellington's victory at Waterloo in 1815. It is a grand viewpoint overlooking Bar Brook and down to Chatsworth. It is also a good place for a rest.

Eaglestone Flat

Across the moor, known as Eaglestone Flat, can be seen the Eagle stone itself. It is an unprepossessing lump of rock, for all the world looking like cowpats piled on top of each other. It deserves the climb. Local folklore has it that no one was allowed to wed a Baslow girl without first climbing the Eagle Stone.

As you approach the Eagle Stone, what seemed simple gradually assumes a different aspect. There is a singular lack of good hand and the footholds and ledges around the rock all seem to slope outwards. It is also one of those rocks which look twice as high when you are on top as when you're on the ground. Retreat from the rock back to the Wellington monument and turn left onto a broad track which carries you down towards Clod Hall cross roads.

The Eagle Stone, with Wellington's Monument in the distance

This track was the Baslow to Sheffield road until 1808 when the present A621 road was built. In the Peak District, most of the main roads we know today came into existence in the 75 years between 1750 and 1825, some on the same lines as packhorse routes but many entirely new. There has never since been such a spate of road building, despite the changes in recent transport systems.

Follow the track down to a gate on the Curbar Gap road and turn right down the road to Clod Hall cross roads. Cross the Bar Brook again in the process. Go over the cross roads and immediately on the right is a stile leading onto the moors again.

A path strikes out almost due south heading for the northern end of Birchens Edge, seen ahead. Other paths deviate right towards Gardoms Edge but ignore these. Continue upwards through scattered birch trees until you are almost level with the rocks. Here the path forks, the easy route going straight on, along the base of the Edge. The left-hand path strikes up through the rocks to reach a trig point on the summit. Go left and scramble up onto the edge. Again, this is a good place for a break to admire the view.

Nelson's Monument

Continue along Birchens Edge, soon reaching Nelson's Monument. This commemorates Nelson's victory at Trafalgar. To reinforce the nautical flavour, the three rocks on top of the edge are called "Three Ships" and are inscribed with the names of ships of Nelson's fleet. Many of the climbs also have nautical associations, such as Powder Monkey Traverse.

Proceed along the edge until the path suddenly dips. Turn sharp right and go down a little gully in the rocks to rejoin the path running at the bottom of the edge. Go left here and follow the path back to the road just above the Robin Hood pub and the car park.

Walk 7: Baslow

The Route: Baslow Nether End, Chatsworth Park, Queen Mary's Bower, Edensor, Paddocks Plantation, Pilsley, Rymas Brook, Baslow West End

Distance: 9 km (6 mls)

Start: Baslow Nether End car park (Grid Reference 258722)

Map: Ordnance Survey Outdoor Leisure No 24 – The Peak District, White Peak Area.

How to get there:

By Bus – There are daily services to Baslow from Chesterfield, Sheffield, Manchester and The Potteries. All stop at Nether End

By Car – Travel on the A621 road from Sheffield, the A619 from Chesterfield, the A623 from Chapel-en-le-Frith, the A619 from Bakewell. The car park is signposted in Baslow.

The Devonshire Arms in Pilsley, nestling in an attractive part of this Chatsworth estate village, is open from 11.00 am until 2.30 pm and from 6.45 pm in the evenings from Mondays – Saturdays. Usual Sunday hours. Those who enjoy a pint of Stones cask or Mansfield Riding or Old Baily bitter will enjoy this pub in particular. A full bar menu is available at lunchtimes and weekday evenings.

The Walk

From Baslow Nether End car park, turn right and go past the bus stops and over the Barbrook Bridge. Then, turn right, following a good path into Chatsworth Park. The Barbrook Bridge originally carried the Chesterfield road into Baslow until it was moved to its present route outside the parkland.

The path joins another route trailing in from the right and bears left, passes through a kissing gate and into open parkland. There follows a mile of easy and delightful walking on paths and estate roads, keeping close to the River Derwent, except where the walled gardens and campsite intervene. To the left, the land rises to the Hunting Tower. At a lower level, Chatsworth House, known as The Palace of the Peak, can be seen clearly.

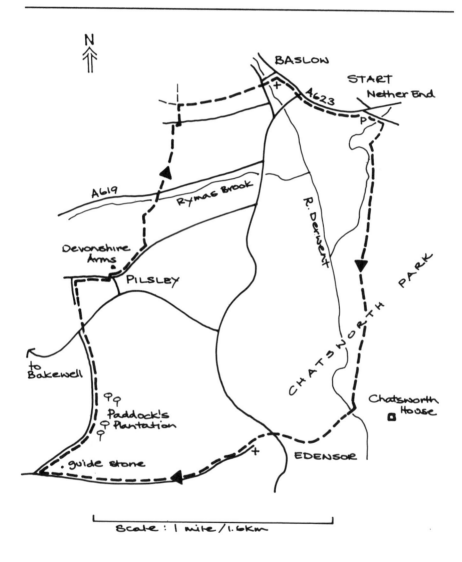

Scale : 1 mile / 1.6km

Chatsworth House

Chatsworth House and Park are one of the Peak District's greatest tourist attraction. They can generate traffic jams in the height of summer so choose when you go. The house and gardens seen today were laid out between 1687 and 1707 on behalf of William Cavendish, the First Duke of Devonshire. The Dukes of Devonshire have lived here ever since and fortunately, this masterpiece is open for public enjoyment.

The route keeps close to the River Derwent until the ruins of Queen Mary's Bower are reached. This structure has links with the tragic Mary Queen of Scots who spent a number of her periods of imprisonment at Chatsworth between 1570 and 1581. The bower is a raised, moated enclosure, approached by a single flight of steps. A delightful spot but an effective way of keeping the queen under control.

Beyond the bower, go right, over the bridge. This bridge was part of the great rebuilding in the last part of the 17th century. Before that, another nearby bridge carried the Bakewell to Chesterfield road over the Derwent. The making of the parkland in the 1690s caused the closure of the road. Just over the bridge bear right, thus leaving the road and head along a path towards the village of Edensor. This path was the alignment of the old road, which soon appears as a terrace as the path rises up the bank and the village comes into view.

Edensor

Cross the main road, which can get busy, and enter the village through the gates. This settlement is owned by the Chatsworth Estates. It was built in the mid-19th century, allegedly for those whose homes were demolished because they happened to spoil the Duke's view. The "new" Edensor is most unusual in design and layout. No two houses are the same. It is entirely surrounded by a wall and fence to prevent straying cattle. The central feature, the church, is impressive, a structure dating from the 1860s to the design of Gilbert Scott and completed in 1870. In the churchyard is the grave of the sister of the late President Kennedy. She was married to the Marquis of Hartington, the eldest son of the sixth Duke.

Go through the village and out up the lane which soon becomes a rough track. This was once the old Chesterfield to Bakewell road. After a mile of easy though uphill climbing, another road is joined. In the angle between the two roads is a guide stone lettered Bakewell Road, Sheffield Road and Chesterfield Road, dated 1709. Turn sharp right here along the "Sheffield" road and descend to the T-junction passing Paddock's Plantation on the right.

At the T-junction go straight across to a stile and into a field. The exit from this is another stile straight ahead on the alignment of the lane you have just walked down, for there was at one time a crossroads here. There is a surprisingly good view from this point, up the Derwent valley towards Higger Tor (at Fox House), Baslow and Curbar Edges. Go over the stile into a rough walled lane. A view opens up to Hassop Common, Longstone Edge and Fin Cop, the latter being recognisable by the plateau-like top and very steep right-hand slope.

The lane bends to the right, the slopes on the left falling away to Rymas Brook with Toost Bank Wood beyond. There was a proposal in the 1960s for a reservoir in the upper valley of Rymas Brook, but it did not materialise. Another narrow lane goes off left, but you keep straight on and soon reach the first houses of Pilsley. The village has a church, shop, post office and public house.

Local Wells

On leaving the pub, go left and continue down the main street soon leaving the village behind. In the garden of the last house on the left is an old grindstone and, opposite, is a white gate which protects a well. This is a reminder that not too long ago most Peak District villages relied heavily on local wells and springs.

Baslow and the Eastern edges are in view as a barn is reached, at which point bear left over an unsigned stile, by a sycamore tree. The path is not at all distinct but keeps alongside a wall, descending gently towards the valley of Rymas Brook. Where the gradient steepens, at the end of the wood, go through a gap in the wall on the right and negotiate a difficult stile designed for gymnasts.

Once over the stile, the path slants steeply down, following the electricity power line. Baslow Edge can be seen prominently ahead. Note on the opposite side of the valley an electricity pole in the field. This is the key to path finding once you are over the road. Follow the power

Looking through the Lych Gate, Baslow church (Courtesy of Chris Rushton)

line down to a well-hidden bridge and stile. Ignore the obvious paths on the right heading down the valley – these are cattle tracks.

Having located the bridge and stile, emerge onto the A619 main road. Cross this busy road with care, and go through a stile opposite. Head upwards towards the pole mentioned earlier and cross the field to the left of a depression to reach a gate in the top right-hand corner. Do not take the obvious path through the right-hand gateway, but go over a stile ahead and follow a boundary wall to the next stile. Head for the wall on the opposite side of the field, then follow it to the left to a stile and road.

Go right here towards Baslow, now seen ahead, then go left at the footpath, which is signed. This crosses the next field to a prominent upright stone in the wall. Here, imperceptibly, there is a crossing of paths. Go right and follow the wall straight down through a series of fields to emerge on the road almost opposite the old bridge over the Derwent. This was the original route to Baslow.

Medieval Bridge

The route crosses a fine medieval bridge, restored in the 17th century. It includes a toll keeper's hut built into the northern parapet. There is some doubt whether this was for the collection of tolls but was certainly used to spy on travellers as they approached the village.

From the bridge, follow the main road round past the church. Note the Jubilee Clock which, instead of numerals, has the word and date VICTORIA 1897. This was the idea of a dedicated resident at the time, a Dr Wrench who, thirty years earlier, organised the building of the Wellington Monument on Baslow Edge. The fact that the 1897 on the clockface is not coincident with the hours 1, 8, 9 or 7 simply adds to the confusion, but this could have been very useful when pub opening hours were more strict! Evidently, one of the artefacts in the church is a dog whip used by one the church elders in previous centuries to chase out stray dogs. Continue on the main road past The Rutland Arms and the roundabout, then over the rise to pass The Cavendish Hotel and down so to the car park and bus stops at Nether End.

Walk 8: Calver

The Route: Calver Bridge, Townend Wood, Bubnell Farm, Oxpasture, Back Wood, Bramley Wood, Calver village

Distance: 7 km (4 mls)

Start: Bridge Inn, Calver Bridge. Car Parking on old road. (Grid Reference 248744).

Map: Ordnance Survey Outdoor Leisure No 24 – The Peak District, The White Peak Area.

How to get there:

By Bus – There is a good daily service from Sheffield and Bakewell as well as from Chesterfield and Manchester.

By Car – From Baslow travel on the A623 to Calver Bridge, where there is a right turn onto the old road just before the bridge. Those travelling from the A6 then the A623 through Sparrowpit and Calver Sough should proceed over Calver Bridge and turn left into the old road.

The Bridge Inn at Calver Bridge is a smashing old pub serving Kimberley ales from Nottinghamshire including their Best Bitter and Kimberley Classic. The pub is open from 11.30 am until 3 pm on Monday to Saturday. Evening hours are from 5.30 pm and 6pm on Saturday. Usual Sunday opening. Bar meals are served at lunchtime and early evening and there's a marvellously large garden for summertime supping which appeals to families in particular.

The Walk

From the pub, go left over the old bridge which spans the River Derwent. On the right, just over the bridge is Calver Mill which featured in the television series "Colditz". Go left under the new road and follow the riverside path over the footbridge across the sough tail and to open fields. A sough (pronounced "suff") is a tunnel for draining a mine.

The Bridge, Calver (Courtesy of Chris Rushton)

Calver Sough drained the mines west of Calver. The water of the sough sees daylight in the village and then runs as a stream to the Derwent.

Continue along the river path to a stile and on again, ignoring paths to the right. The path keeps close to the Derwent, with views across to Baslow Edge. At a stile by the bend in the river the path enters a wood and begins to draw away from the river bank. Leaving the wood the path runs as a short section of walled lane to a point where the two gates with a stile between them present a choice. The stile happens to be the correct route. This remnant lane is probably the route leading to the ancient river crossing of Stanton Ford, whence the packhorse way climbed over Curbar Gap and onto the moors. Curbar Edge can be seen as you look back.

Go through a stile and then diagonally across a field to another stile on the left of a gate. Here a rough road is joined and there is a good example of a stone-lined spring and trough. Bear left at the road and follow this, up the hill at first, towards Bubnell. At the 30MPH road sign, go right up a little lane, passing Bubnell Grange on the left. Where the lane bears right to Bubnell Farm, there is a signpost pointing left which directs you through a gateway into a field alongside the Grange. It is tempting to go straight ahead as the way is not obvious here, but you turn right and march up the middle of the field to a gateway half-way along the far wall.

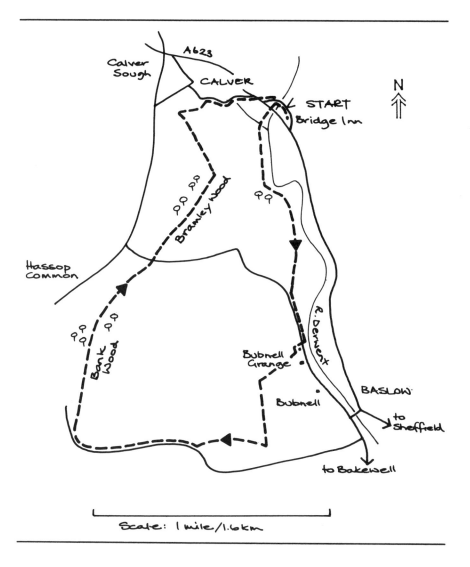

The way is not obvious underfoot at this point. From the gateway, the Hunting Tower at Chatsworth can be seen to the left. The path, according to the map, turns right part-way up the next field to reach the second gateway on the left. In practice, local walkers cut the corner to the gate. Go through it and pause to look back. The view up the valley is extensive, with the Eastern edges particularly prominent.

Follow the wall on the left to a stile to the left of a gate. Baslow is now in full view to the left. Go over a stile and continue along a wall to the corner, which is in the middle of a field! Here, turn right and head up the field. There is no obvious path, but keep ahead to a stile in the top right-hand corner of the field to the right of a trough. Cross the stile and keep straight on with a wall on the right, to another stile at the top of the field. Go over this stile and follow the wall again to a corner where, according to the map, there should be a wall running towards the little barn and another crossing the line of march. Neither of these exists now, so head straight on towards the barn. When you top the rise, bear left across the field to a gateway in the far left corner. This leads onto a narrow lane.

Roman Origins

This lane is ancient and was once the main road from Chesterfield to Buxton and Manchester. It may have Roman origins, lying in an excellent alignment between fortresses at Chesterfield and Buxton and linking Roman settlements south of Monsal Dale. It was one of the early turnpikes until superseded by the present main road through Stoney Middleton. Go right, along the lane until it tops the rise at the north end of Toost Wood. The lane bears right and descends. Where it levels out, a signpost on the right directs you through a stile by a gate into a rough field.

The exit from the field lies up to the left over a rickety stile. The path now goes into Bank Wood. The path is clear underfoot, twisting its way through the wood, always keeping close to a wall on the right. Emerging from the wood, you can see Oxpasture Farm below on the left, while to the right there are views over the wall to the Eastern edges. Across the valley to the left is Hassop Common, an area extensively worked for lead and fluorspar. Backdale Mine can be clearly seen and the noise of its workings is all too obvious from now on.

Boundary Markers

The path goes back into woodland again and according to the map carries on alongside the wall to the road. In practice, there is a stile on the right which is easily missed. Go over this and then turn left along a good track, which soon goes down to a gate onto the road. Bear left here and, almost at once, go right, through a rickety gate into Bramley Wood. There are glimpses to Chatsworth, to the Eastern edges, to Sir William Hill with its mast and to Ladywash with its chimney. Every so often there are unusual concrete cubes by the path. They appear to be boundary markers but to what purpose? As you walk there is an increasing sense of height and the realisation as Calver appears below, that the descent is going to short and sharp.

Eventually, the path begins to descend and at a second sign post go left down a steepening track. At the next signpost go right, leaving the track and descending steeply through scrub to a stile which leads into open fields. Continue to descend, ignoring gates leading into fields to the right and cross a muddy area by the spring. Climb away from the spring up the field, bearing half right to the hawthorn and the stile in the wire fence. Continue straight on with a wall to the right. The paths are not clear here, but you bear right through a gap in the wall. The path soon comes to the backs of houses where a stile on the left drops onto what looks like a private drive. Turn left to follow the drive to the main village street opposite Pennine Cottage and go right, along the road. Where the footpath for Bubnell leaves on the right, look out for the outlet of Calver Sough. Follow the street to the main road. Cross it and go down the footway to the Bridge Inn, passing Calver Craft centre on the left.

Walk 9: Eyam

The Route: Highcliffe, Broad Low, Sir William Hill, Ladywash, Beech Hurst

Distance: 6km (4 mls)

Start: Eyam Church (Grid Reference 218765).

Map: Ordnance Survey Outdoor Leisure 24 – The Peak District, White Peak Area

How to get there:

By Bus – Eyam is served daily by buses from Sheffield and Buxton. There is a bus stop by the church.

By Car – From the west travel on the A6 then the A623 road and at Middleton Dale be vigilant for a turning left signposted to Eyam. From the east travel from Calver on the A623 then take the first turn right after Stoney Middleton. There are a car park and toilets in Hawkhills Road in Eyam and the walk can be started there instead of the church.

The Bull's Head stands opposite the church in a fine group of buildings including the Mechanics Institute. The Bull's Head has enjoyed several name changes. It used to be called The Talbot Inn in 1606 but the original building was raised to the ground by fire. In 1710 it was renamed the Bull's Head. This large inn offers accommodation and has a lounge and smoke room, the latter having a welcoming fire in the winter.

Several of the local customers enjoy pool in a back area. Food is generally not served, but Youngers and Theakstons draught beer is available on handpull. The Bull's Head is open noon until 3 pm on Mondays to Fridays and from 7 pm in the evenings. It is open all day on Saturday and usual hours on Sunday. It is also handy for the bus stop outside.

The Bull's Head (Courtesy of Chris Rushton)

Plague Village

In the 1660s a plague struck middle England with a vengance bringing death and grief to many rural areas. In 1665, it hit the village of Eyam and the populace decided to impose a quarantine on itself to stop the plague spreading to other communities. The effect was devastating – the disease took 259 lives, often wiping out entire families. The poignant story is recalled by plaques and memorials throughout Eyam.

The Old Hall, Eyam (Courtesy of Chris Rushton)

The Walk

Start from the church, which is a fascinating reflection of social history, having been renovated by many communities throughout the centuries. Victor Mompesson was the rector of the parish at the time of the plague and rallied the parishioners to stay and bear the disease. His wife's tomb is to be found in the churchyard near to the old Saxon cross. Nearby is an unusual sundial dating from 1775.

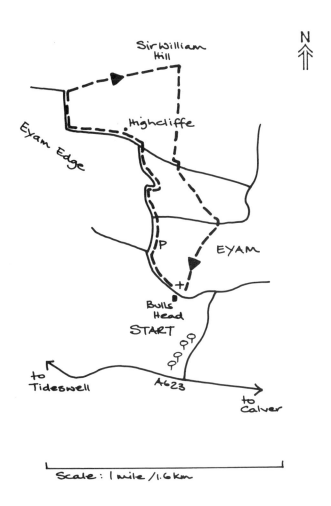

From the entrance to the churchyard turn right to pass the plague cottages, and the Old Hall. Opposite, there is a small village green with stocks and information board. Further along, turn right into Hawkhill Road, signposted to the Youth Hostel, to pass by the new toilet block. Follow this up to the corner where the main road bears right. You, however, go left up a road which climbs steeply past houses and becomes a zig-zag rough track. This eventually reaches a road near to Highcliffe.

Eyam Edge

Turn left here and continue to climb above Eyam Edge. The road bends sharp right and goes along a short straight section up to another junction. Bear right here along a wide track, climbing to Sir William Hill, a name said to honour Sir William Cavendish from nearby Stoke Hall in the 17th century. This is not without contention, for some reckon the name honours a Sir William Saville then of the Manor of Eyam! Couldn't it be to both? Whatever, the views are spectacular across The Peak District.

Ladywash

Just beyond the summit, as the track begins to descend look for a ladder stile on the right. Cross it and keep ahead with a drystone wall on your left through fields to a stile before exiting onto a road. To the left is Ladywash, one of the many old lead mines found in this area. At the road, go left for 30 to 40 paces and then turn right to cross a stile. The path leads slightly left down the field to cross a stile in the field corner. It then curves left above banks of bracken to dip right to a stile above a wood. Cross the stile and walk alongside a wall.

Keep ahead to a stile and then cut right, down a steep bank to follow a well-worn path left, still near to a wall. The path drops down to a stile and a lovely set of stone steps. Cross the road, go left for a few paces and then turn right over a stone step-stile by a gate. Follow the well-trodden path down the hill to a stile where you bear right. The path now bends right, following a drystone wall on the left as it descends to a gap-stile. Keep ahead again through the old workings and onto a track. Then proceed towards the churchyard. Enter it through a gateway and pass by the church to the road and The Bull's Head.

Walk 10: Foolow

The Route: Hucklow Edge, Abney Grange, Great Hucklow, Grindlow

Distance: 7 km (4 mls)

Start: The Lazy Landlord, Foolow (Grid Reference 192768).

Map: Ordnance Survey 24 The Peak District – White Peak Area

How to get there:

By Bus – Foolow is served daily by the Sheffield to Buxton via Eyam bus.

By Car – Travel on the A623 and at Houseley between Stoney Middleton and Wardlow Mires, look for a turning signposted off to Foolow. There is limited car parking in Foolow, near the pond, so please park considerately.

The Lazy Landlord is a split level pub. It has a central bar serving one of the nicest pints of Ward's beer for miles around. One part of the bar is thought to have been the old stables of this roadside inn and is often frequented by ramblers. The other side of the bar is more of a restaurant.

The less-than-lazy landlord serves from 11.30 am until 2.30 pm and from 6 pm in the evenings from Monday to Saturday, and usual hours on Sunday. Food is also served lunchtimes and mid evening. The pub was previously known more traditionally as The Bull's Head. One thing is for certain, everyone remembers the newer name and the pub sign is a work of art.

The Walk

From The Lazy Landlord, turn right and then right again by the chapel, on the road signposted to Bretton. Pass the well and then a drive to an isolated farmstead on the left. As the road bends to the right leave it for the fields. Cross a step-stile on the left (signposted) and walk up a long field with a dry stone wall to the right. Cross the stile and go straight on. The path leads to a wooden stile which is crossed and then on to rough ground. Go left to climb a steep bank, being the transition to gritstone.

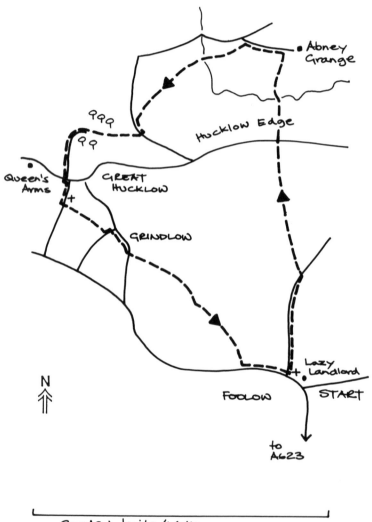

Scale : 1 mile/1.6km

Hucklow Edge

You come to a more dominant cross-track, but keep ahead here to cross a stile and climb, climb, climb up Hucklow Edge. Cross the road and take a deep-breath, admiring the view from this vantage point. Then, keep ahead over a stile. The path is signposted – you soon feel a sense of elation as you begin to drop into a steep-sided valley. The path has been eroded in places so steps have been provided as it is a sharp descent in places, and not a spot for vertigo sufferers. The path leads down to a bridge across the infant brook.

Abney Grange

It then begins to climb to the right between bracken and a crumbling dry stone wall. At the top of the enclosure, bear left up to a stile which is crossed. Take a breather, for the climb is quite a tall order. Continue to climb up the hill with a dry stone wall to your right. Towards the top go right, over a stile and walk along the edge of the field, the farm buildings of Grange Farm at Abney Grange coming closer. Do not enter the farm but keep to the left where there is a stone stile exiting onto a road.

Go left and climb to a junction with another road coming in from the right. Just beyond the junction, go over a stile on the left by a gate and head very slightly left across the field. Cross a stile by the gate in the top far left corner and then the path follows a wall back down into the clough. Climb the hill on the other side with a dry stone wall to the left and soon cross a ladder stile. Then proceed ahead, keeping just to the left of the building now seen in the dip, where a stile is crossed.

Great Hucklow

Pass to the left of the building and climb the bank which leads up to a stile and road. Turn left and begin to walk down the hill with a reservoir to the left. As the road enters a wood and bears left, go right down a lovely woodland track. This curves left to pass by a school and becomes a road which leads to Great Hucklow, known for its gliding club. Those seeking a mid-walk pint should turn right for The Queen Anne, a cosy little village pub a few minutes walk away.

Otherwise at the junction in the village turn left and then first right. Just past the Unitarian chapel, founded 1696, rebuilt 1796 and enlarged 1901, go left over a stile and pass through two small enclosures behind a farm. Keep ahead through two more enclosures to pass by another farm. Go through one of the narrowest gap stiles in the world, and then pass through the bottom of a garden onto the road.

Turn left here and then right at the road junction by Chapel House Farm stables. The road leads to other houses and bends right. At this point keep ahead along a green track, passing between a house garden and a barn. Follow the walled green lane back into the White Peak, characterised by a sea of limestone walls. The lane eventually gives out at a gap-stile into a field. Go very slightly right, across this field to another gap-stile. In the next small enclosure, bear right to cross a track and stone step-stile back to the road. Turn left for the short walk back into Foolow.

The Lazy Landlord, Foolow

Walk 11: Rainow

The Route: Rainow, Back of Gin Clough,The Highwayman, Moss Brook. Blue Boar, Billinge Hill, Rainowlow.

Distance: 4 km (2.5 mls)

Start: Rainow Church. Map Reference 953759.

There is limited on-street parking off the main road in Rainow, but please park considerately. Alternatively, start from a lay-by on the road to Lamaload Reservoir near Pike Low, around the corner from The Highwayman pub (Map Reference 966768).

Map: Ordnance Survey Outdoor Leisure No 24 – The Peak District, White Peak Area.

How to get there:

By Bus – There is a daily service from Macclesfield to Rainow which is frequent on Mondays to Saturdays. There are five journeys on Sunday afternoons which fit in well with a walk.

By Car – Travel on the A5004 between Whaley Bridge and Macclesfield to Rainow. Limited parking as mentioned above.

The Highwayman is a very appropriately named pub as the area was renowned for its footpads and highwaymen in earlier times. One famous gang used to hang out at nearby Pym's Chair (a possible derivation of the name) and spy on the waggons climbing from the Cheshire plains into hill country. A modern-day highwayman dressed in black has occasionally called into the pub to entertain groups of visitors. This was much to the consternation of one elderly local who shook his head disapprovingly on his way to the Gents muttering "Aye lad, it's a long time since we've seen you in these parts."

The Highwayman is open Mondays to Saturday from noon to approximately 2.30/3 pm and from 7 pm in the evenings. Usual Sunday hours. It sells a cracking pint of Thwaites traditional bitter and homemade food. Children are welcome at lunchtimes only, as there are no facilities for families in the evening. There are a few seats in the front

*The authors in conference at
The Highwayman*

of the pub which offer a superb view of Cheshire on a summer evening.

The Walk

Start opposite the entrance to Rainow church on the main Macclesfield road. Rainow used to be something of a small township because it had so many mills fed by the River Dean. It is said that Rainow once had its own mayor and, at his inauguration ceremony, he, was expected to ride backwards and blindfolded on a donkey between each pub. That could be taking mayoral duties a little too far. Virtually all of the mills have disappeared with the exception of Gin Clough Mill on the way to the Highwayman pub. One of the best walking books covering this locality is "The Industrial Revolution in East Cheshire: Six Theme walks" by George Longden. The author includes several very old photographs of mills that have long-since gone.

Stocks

Walk up the main road to pass by the shop and soon after, a road bears off left. Go left here, but then immediately right, up Stocks Lane, to pass by some old houses. At the rear of the village hall, pass the stocks to a junction with Smithy Lane, where the Macclesfield bus turns round. Just beyond is the Robin Hood public house. This is very welcoming, should you become thirsty on the outward or return leg of the ramble. The pub serves the Greenall Whitley range of draught beers, nowadays brewed by a large combine on their behalf,

Follow Smithy Lane past houses and then by a farmhouse on the left as the road dips to a triangular junction. Look out for the ducks in the stream here. Bear right and begin to climb the hill. Opposite the barn of Lower House, turn right to go over a stile as signposted (but the sign is likely to be at knee level unless someone hoists it up again by the time you walk by).

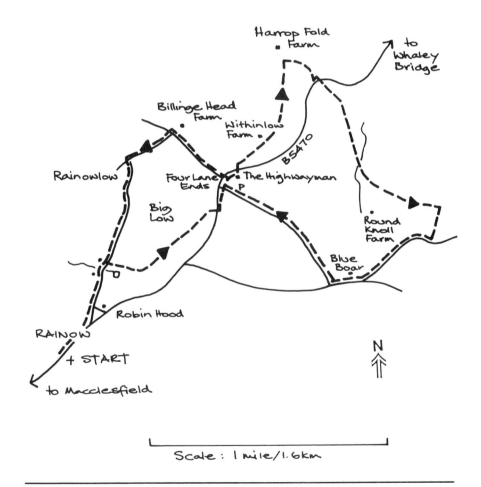

Scale : 1 mile/1.6km

Pass by a reservoir, which is now a fishing pool. In the last century, this was the water supply for one of the many mills in Rainow which flourished until the rise of Macclesfield and Bollington with their larger, steam-powered mills.

White Nancy

Cross a stile by a hollybush. Then follow a wall on the right by an old barn, to cross another stone stile. Thus, move closer to a stream on the right. Walk ahead along the stream bank for a matter of twenty or thirty paces to meet another path crossing here. Bear left to climb a sunken green path rising up the hillside to a stone step-stile. Cross this and keep ahead to shortly cross another. The views over the Dean Valley to Kerridge Ridge, crowned with the White Nancy monument, are excellent from this vantage point.

Keep company with the dry stone wall on the left as it climbs higher to another stone stile, this time with extremely large stone steps. Once over, proceed to a stile by a pole. Then bear left to cross a wooden stile and continue across a ladder stile. All these are easily seen when walking through these small enclosures. Proceed ahead through a gateway and onto a stone step-stile, to the left of two stone gateposts. Continue ahead to a wooden fence protecting a stone stile, which deposits you onto the main road, so take care to look right before placing one step further. Cross the road and walk facing the traffic for a short distance to a junction.

The Highwayman

On the right, the road leads to Lamaload. If you attempt the longer circuit you will return along this section. The lay-by for parking (mentioned in the introduction) is a little way up on the right. The main road ahead, curves gently right to The Highwayman pub, so press on for a tasty pint of Thwaites.

Those seeking an early cut-off point should progress to the paragraph headed *Billinge Hill*.

Harrop Valley

On the left, opposite the pub, is a stone step-stile by a footpath signpost down a low wall to a track. This is very awkward, so some people simply walk through the gate instead. There is a barn on the left and the track continues ahead to a gap-stile by a barred gate. In the next field, go through a stone gap stile and keep in much the same direction to pass near to Withinlow Farm on the left. The track becomes more of an old green way now. Keep ahead to cross a stone step-stile to the right of a gate. Join a line of hawthorns and you soon cross another stone step-stile in a broken dry stone wall. It might be better to dip to the left of this as it is a little precarious. Go straight on to cross a wooden stile, a drive and a stone step-stile to enter a field. Continue to a ladder stile before Harrop Fold Farm.

Once on the drive, turn right, away from the farm and climb back to the main road. Cross the road with caution here and then go along a drive opposite, towards what look like barns. There is a dwelling here too however. Just before the buildings, take the lesser, lower track which skirts to the left of a silage compound. This track follows the fence on the left along a tractor track towards a gateway and assorted tangled metal.

Moss Brook

Peel off left before the gateway along an old track. The ground is wetter as you follow this to a wooden stile which is crossed. A path joins here by way of a stile on your left. Your way is however, slightly right through rough ground, into the valley of the Moss Brook. The path keeps straight along the hillside and then begins to drop to the stream, where another stile is crossed.

Once over, cross the stream and begin to climb out of the gully. Head up the bank to join a wall, with Round Knoll Farm ahead across the pasture. This is sheep farming territory, where cases of sheep-rustling have been reported in recent years! Keep ahead now, up the field known as Saddle Cote and cross stiles and a wall. Continue ahead, descending gently to the field corner, rather than crossing the stile near the summit on the right. At the corner, cross a stile by the gate and go straight ahead with a dry stone wall to the left. There's a good view of Pym's Chair and Shining Tor from here. In the valley is Jenkin Chapel, a humble place of worship built by local farmsteads centuries ago. Despite rural de-population in these parts, monthly services are still held.

Old Blue Boar

Leave the field by a stile next to a gate and join an old track, almost certainly a salter's way, and used for motor scrambles before the Second World War. Go right and the track soon becomes a metalled road. At the junction with the road to Lamaload, bear right to pass Old Blue Boar Farm, which was at one time an inn. At the next junction beyond, bear right and walk up the hill. There are some great views across to Charles Head and beyond. You then walk down again to pass the lay-by and head back to Four Lane Ends.

Billinge Hill

Cross the road and turn left down the Bollington road with views over Cheshire. At the bottom of the hill pass by Billinge Head Farm, with Billinge Hill beyond, which at one time was quarried extensively. Turn next left along a track by a wood. This track passes a house and soon curves right, to rise up gently. At the junction, bear left along a higher lane, to pass homesteads and the scars of a small, old quarry, one of many surface workings which have extracted gritstone from these foothills. Beneath is the isolated hamlet of Rainowlow, no more than a huddle of houses, but it has retained a distinct identity from the nearby larger village.

Big Low

The track becomes a metalled road as it climbs and falls beneath Big Low – a seeming contradiction, but 'low' means 'high ground' in this context! The road joins the T-junction encountered earlier and returns to The Robin Hood and bus stop. Is there time to adjourn before the journey home?

Walk 12: Goyt Valley

The Route: Fernilee Reservoir, Fernilee, The Shady Oak, Folds End, Goyt, Deep Clough

Distance: 9 km (6 mls)

Start: Car park by side of Errwood Reservoir (Grid Reference 014757)

Map: Ordnance Survey Outdoor Leisure 24 – The Peak District, White Peak Area

How to get there:

By Bus – The walk must be started from The Shady Oak, which is served Mondays to Saturdays from Whaley Bridge

By Car – Travel on the A5002 from Whaley Bridge to Buxton. Goyt Valley is signposted from this road.

The Shady Oak at Fernilee is a pleasant looking hostelry with a Victorian post box and North Western bus stop. For years, it has been a stopping-off point for travellers on Long Hill, a very apposite name for the road. The pub was at one time an old staging house for horse drawn transport. It belonged to an old brewery, Clarkes of Stockport until taken over by Boddingtons. Ironically, two of the North West's favourite beverages, Boddingtons Mild and Bitter, are no longer brewed by Boddingtons but belong to the giant Whitbread. Production still occurs at the famous Strangeways brewery and the brand name will no doubt persist.

The Shady Oak has two rooms, a tap room on the left and a long lounge geared up very much for food. Both are served by a long bar, and mild and bitter are available on draught. From Monday to Saturday, opening hours are 1130 am to 3 pm, reopening at 7 pm. On Saturday the pub re-opens at 5.30 pm. Food is served at lunchtimes and evenings. Usual Sunday hours prevail.

The Shady Oak (Courtesy of Chris Rushton)

The Walk

From the car park at Errwood cross the dam between the two reservoirs, Errwood on the right and Fernilee to the left. Errwood was opened as late as 1968, with an average daily quantity of water supplied being 17 million gallons to the Stockport area. The reservoir also forms the basis of leisure activity with a thriving sailing club.

At the end of the dam bear left down an access road towards the right-hand bank of Fernilee reservoir. Join the old trackbed of the Cromford and High Peak Railway. Part of the old track is now the road down Bunsal Cob. It was a most peculiar railway – the incline was so steep that train loads were hauled up or down by a stationary steam engine.

Hotbed

The setting seems so tranquil now, but during the last century this valley was a hotbed of industrialisation with quarrying, coal mining, paint

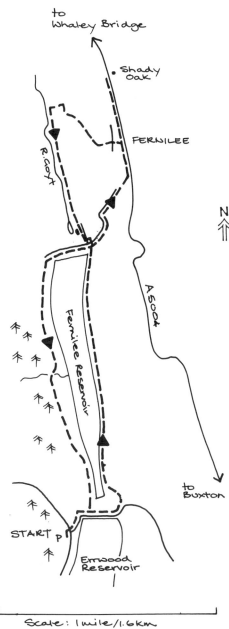

to
Whaley Bridge

Shady
Oak

FERNILEE

R.Goyt

N

A5004

Fernilee Reservoir

to
Buxton

START P

Errwood
Reservoir

Scale: 1 mile/1.6km

production and gunpowder. Lying beneath the still waters of Fernilee is the Chilworth gunpowder factory, which came to a tragic end when it blew up in 1909, killing three employees.

Shady Oak

Follow the track for the length of the reservoir and at the end turn right onto a road by a house. This leads to Fernilee and the main road. Turn left here and walk along to The Shady Oak for mid-walk refreshment. Leave the pub and retrace your steps on the right-hand side, facing the traffic. Pass the telephone kiosk and, opposite Elnor Lane, go right by Ivy Cottage and walk down a small valley under the bridge to join another track. Keep ahead and soon, at a wall between junctions, go to the left. Then in a few paces bear right, over a stone stile by Fernilee Cottages.

The path is now coralled and heads slightly right to cross a stile. Keep to the hedge on the right and proceed through a gateway. Go right, over the next stile, then cut across rough ground to another stile above a stream. Cross the stile and follow the path as it curves around to the left and down to a stile which is also crossed. Head for the footbridge over the River Goyt, but do not go over it. Instead, turn left up the valley with the Goyt on the right, a delightful unpolluted river at this stage of its life.

The path soon becomes a track up to the waterworks. Pass the first buildings on the left and then turn left before the next building. The road climbs up the side of the sluice to a junction. Go right to the top of the dam and walk along it. The view down the Goyt is excellent, the trees all manner of shades in autumn.

Silent Wood

Go left at the end of the dam and then very shortly, at the corner, left again over a stile into woodland. This well worn path is easy to follow. In the wood keep ahead at the old wooden seat, then cross the bridge in Deep Clough. Walk through silent woodland to Jep Clough and closer to the reservoir. Cross the tall ladder stile and climb away from the wood and across the pasture to the road by Errwood and head back to the car park.

Walk 13: Millthorpe

The Route: Shillito Wood car park, Ramsley Reservoir, Bar Brook, Car Top, Smeekley Wood, Ewford Bridge, Millthorpe, Johnnygate, Rumbling Street, Crowhole, Barlow Grange, Grange Lumb, Moorhall

Distance: 14 km (9 mls)

Start: Shillito Wood Car Park, Grid reference 295748 (Public Transport users should start at Millthorpe)

Map: Ordnance Survey Outdoor Leisure 24 – The Peak District, White Peak Area

How to get there:

By Bus – A Monday to Saturday service from Chesterfield to Millthorpe. Seasonal Sunday service from Chesterfield to Millthorpe. Also, a daily service from Sheffield and The Potteries to Owler Bar

By Car – Travel on the A621 from Sheffield or Baslow (Golden Gates roundabout). Shillito Wood car park is signed from just north of Clod Hall Lane crossroads.

The Royal Oak at Millthorpe serves Wards and Darleys bitter on handpump. The pub is open weekdays from 11.30 until 2.30 pm (except Mondays) and from 5.30 pm in the evening. Usual Sunday hours. Bar snacks and meals are available. There are seats outside as well as in the beer garden. Delightful in summer.

The stone-built pub, reminiscent of an old toll house, dates from the 17th century. There are two rooms, a cosy nook by the entrance and another room to the right off the bar. Both have open fires in winter and are popular with diners.

The Walk

Leave Shillito Wood car park, go left and walk down to the junction, bearing right there. At the junction you might notice on the right a stump of an old cross, one of several remaining on the Eastern Moors of the Peak District. The crosses were erected as guide stones on what were

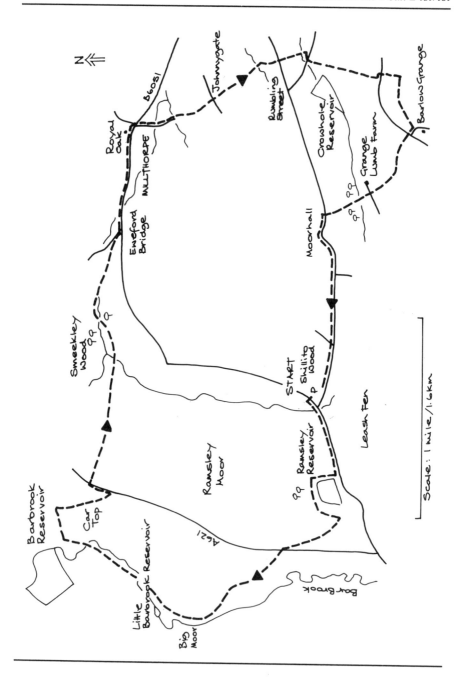

difficult and dangerous routes. Hard to believe, but in the 16th and 17th centuries, guides were required to lead travellers over the inhospitable moors, such routes being described as "miry and founderous".

On the opposite side of the road is Leash Fen, reputedly the site of a market, as the old adage reads:

When Chesterfield was gorse and broom then Leash Fen was a market town
Now Leash Fen is but gorse and broom and Chesterfield the market town.

It all sounds unlikely, but historians suggest that the moors were well-populated in the Bronze Age when Chesterfield was uncleared forest.

The Royal Oak (Courtesy of Chris Rushton)

Bee Warning

Continue along the wide verge next to the road until a gate on the right marks the way onto Ramsley Moor. Go over the stile, noting the bee warning and enter the National Park's Eastern Moors estate. Wildlife has been encouraged during the past few years, particularly in the special sanctuary areas (so, please respect them).

Follow the path round the reservoir, through the alder wood. Be careful to bear left at the signpost pointing to Barbrook Valley and soon join a good path. There's a good view to Big Moor, Gardoms and Birchen's Edges, the Eagle Stone and Wellington Monument rounds the corner into Barbrook valley. The packhorse routes coming over from Baslow and Curbar are clearly seen as deep trenches descending to cross the Barbrook just near the crossroads. Far away on the horizon can be seen the distinctive tuft of trees on Minninglow hill.

Bronze Age Relics

The track soon reaches the A621 road, where there is a stile by a gate. Cross the road with care as the traffic travels too fast for comfort here. Go over the stile opposite onto Big Moor. The Ordnance Survey map marks a number of antiquities on this moor, including field systems, stone circles and enclosures. These are but a few of the Bronze Age relics that have been found here, for this moor was thickly populated in prehistoric times. It is a salutary thought, as you gaze across the stream and heather, that humans have made their mark on these moors for thousands of years. The remains are all but swallowed in the encroaching vegetation.

The track follows the line of a culvert, for the moors have been for years in the ownership of water authorities. This has protected them from modern farming practices. Soon Little Barbrook reservoir is reached with its diminutive Duck Island. The track continues over the Barbrook on a bridge. Despite the obvious human tracks, there is a surprisingly isolated feel to the area, yet one of the busiest roads in the Peak District is only about 600 metres away. Keep on up the track towards Barbrook reservoir and water treatment works. Parts of this are derelict and the entire complex will be surplus to requirements soon. Go over a bridge, then follow the path as signposted to the right along the tarmac drive.

Car Top

Shortly another path crosses and there is a further signpost. Go right here along a narrow path, leaving the metalled lane behind. The path heads over Car Top to the A621 road again. Go left here and then shortly turn right, down a narrow rough lane which pursues an almost dead straight course down the hill towards the tree crowned Smeekley Hill. The view is extensive, right over Chesterfield to the limestone ridge where Bolsover Castle stands defiantly.

Ignore all turns left or right. Continue down the track to pass Smeekley Farm, then, just over a stream, turn left along a path which is signposted. This runs by the stream through delightful mixed woodland. Follow the broadening path down by the stream to a crossing of paths. Go straight on here and leave the woodland behind. A footbridge alongside a ruined stone bridge takes you to the main road after a final length of field path. Go straight on along the road, which has little verge beyond Eweford bridge until a footway is gained near Cordwell Farm. This takes you unerringly to the pub at Millthorpe.

Once refreshed, go over the road towards the cafe. Then turn right, down a narrow lane to a ford over the Millthorpe Brook. There is a footbridge here for the faint at heart but the stream is often no more than a trickle. After the ford, the "road" goes right to a farm, but the right of way lies straight ahead. It is an unusual survival. There are two parallel routes here, separated only by a hedge. The lower route is a bridleway, well used by horses and often muddy. The left-hand route is higher and drier for those on foot. This arrangement was not uncommon in packhorse days. Both routes rejoin again at Johnnygate, but the views are better from the path. The path meets the bridleway at a large gate by the farm and stables and both continue to a road.

Barlow Commonside

Cross the road and go over a stile. Drop down by the side of a hedge to a wood where the path bears first right, then left to a stile leading into open fields. Go through a gateway ahead and keeping the hedge to your left, descend to a little stream, with a view left over towards Baslow Commonside. Beyond the stream, the track rises through a cutting, right then left across a field to reach the delightfully named Rumbling Street and another road. Cross the road and continue straight on, noting the stone toadstools, fanciful wind vane and pond and with Bole Hill rising to the left.

Crowhole

Crowhole reservoir can be seen to the right as the path descends alongside a hedge to a stile, then continues down to the corner of the hedge. Look for a waymark on the tree on the right, which points to a well-hidden bridge across Crowhole Brook. This is not at all obvious! Beyond the stream the path ascends to a stile by a holly tree and meets a road. Go right at the road, then left through a gate to follow the wall up into open fields. The path then crosses the field diagonally, to the right of the second electricity pole. Continue to a stile in the wall to the right of a solitary bush. It is quite a pull up this field, but the view over to Sheffield and Holmsfield offers ample reward. The path continues upwards to a stile in the centre of the far wall, then runs alongside the hedge to another stile onto a road.

Go left, then right here, around the buildings. The path is signposted through the yard to a gate into a broad walled lane. This descends to a large ash tree, at which point there is the most difficult technical problem on the entire walk. How do you climb the stile on the right without encountering the guardian holly bush? Once in the field follow the hedge up towards the electricity pole. At this point, the Ordnance Survey map shows a field boundary that has now gone. Go straight across the field and head towards Barlow Grange, crossing a step-stile to the left of the fence. Now keeping the wall on your left, head up the field to another stile which is crossed. Watch out for frisky horses in this field. At this point the buildings of Barlow Grange are on your left and you join a narrow road leading to the house. Go right here to the cross roads and straight across to a walled track.

The track soon enters fields. There is a stile here and the path then runs alongside a wall to another stile. Here, the path veers right towards Grange Lumb Farm and goes through a gap in the hedge into another field. The next stile is in the wall close to the silage clamp of Grange Lumb Farm.

Having negotiated this stile, the farm access is crossed and the path continues ahead to another squeezer stile in the wall surrounding Grange Wood. Once inside the wood, the path descends steeply to a footbridge over Crowhole Brook, then climbs equally steeply out the other side to a stile and open fields. Grange Wood is situated in Grange Lumb, the place name 'Lumb' meaning 'steep-sided wooded valley'. The word occurs quite frequently in Derbyshire and curiously the same or similar meaning is ascribed to a similar-sounding word in Chinese and Japanese!

Moorhall

Press on up the field, ignoring paths to the left and right, heading to the right of the tops of two trees. As the rise is surmounted a stile comes into view with its stones at a very drunken angle. Now head to the right of the buildings and another stile, from where the path dips to join a road running up from Rumbling Street. This is Moorhall. Go left here along the lane, which is followed without deviation for about one mile back to Shillito Wood. As the wood is reached go right and leave the lane, preferring instead the waymarked path past the fine medieval cross into the rear of the car park

Walk 14: Bollington

The Route: Middlewood Way, Macclesfield Canal, Kerridge old tramway, Kerridge Ridge, Waulkmill, Ingersley Hall, Sowcar

Distance: 7 km (4 mls)

Start: The Vale Inn public house (Grid Reference 932781)

Map: Ordnance Survey Outdoor Leisure 24 – The Peak District, White Peak

How to get there:

By Bus – Bollington is well served by bus every day of the week. Ask for the Dog and Partridge, which is two minutes walk from the start point.

By Car – Travel on the B5090 from the Macclesfield Relief Road to Bollington. Turn left into Adlington Road before the Dog and Partridge public house in Bollington village. There is a public car park on the left before The Vale Inn.

The Vale sells an exceptionally good pint of Thwaites Mild and Bitter and an even better pint of Timothy Taylors Landlord. It has secured a place in The Good Beer Guide (and a host of other publications) for a number of years now. Set in a terrace row, the Vale has become increasing popular with walkers and cyclists using the Middlewood Way.

It is an open-plan pub broken up with arches made of locally quarried stone, most probably from Kerridge hill and Tegg's Nose. Food is served during the best part of opening hours except Sunday and Monday evenings. The Vale, as it is known locally, is open 11.30 until 3 pm, Tuesdays to Saturdays (closed Monday lunchtime) and from 7 pm in the evenings. Usual Sunday hours. The pub is packed with jazz fans on Monday evenings as the pub is renowned locally for its jazz and ale evenings. Just the thing to finish off an evening walk!

Bollington from White Nancy

The Walk

From the entrance of the Vale Inn turn left and walk to the car park and childrens play area. Just beyond are steps up to the Middlewood Way, which crosses the impressive Bollington Viaduct, once part of the railway between Macclesfield and Marple.

Turn left to walk along the viaduct, much loved by Bollington residents who campaigned in recent years for its restoration when it was proposed to knock it down. Follow the Way until a road is met, Grimshaw Lane. Turn left and then cross the road to visit the Adelphi Visitor Centre and Cycle Hire, part of the Macclesfield Groundwork Trust. Behind stands the Adelphi Mill. You should see the large stone base of the chimney that once stood by this steam-powered cotton mill, dating from the 1850s. Thankfully, the mill is now used as offices, workshops and a leisure facility.

Macclesfield Canal

Walk up the steps on the left to the Macclesfield canal towpath. Bear right and walk along the canalside past the mill and shortly leave the navigation at Bridge 28 up a fine set of stone steps. Go left over the bridge and continue ahead along a track, ignoring the track to the left. Pass Bobbin Cottage, the name reflecting an old bobbin works that stood here in the last century. Walk by a small wood. At the very next hedge look for a stile on the right. Go over it and walk ahead to a stone gap-stile and then slightly right to go through another, often surrounded by wet ground in winter. Proceed to another stile and then join an old track running straight up from a canal basin seen to the right. This was the Kerridge tramway.

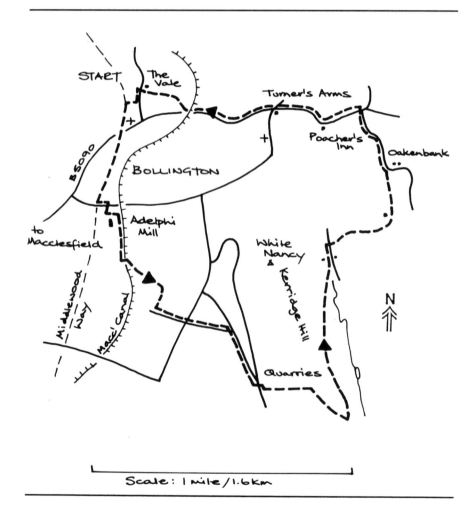

Scale: 1 mile/1.6km

Old Tram Road

Go left to follow the old Kerridge tramway up the incline to Kerridge. The tram road was built in the 1830s to transport stone from Kerridge quarries to the canal. Cross Clarke Lane and continue ahead as the incline steepens, through the gateway to Endon House. You go up the drive to Endon Cottage, where the last stretch of the tramway used to rise under the bridge. The place looks tranquil now, but it was the scene of intense industrial activity a hundred years ago. Kerridge stone is still quarried, but the small quantities of stone are now despatched by road.

However, your way is to turn right before Endon Cottage, up the drive. This leads to a road. Cross this and walk ahead towards the entrance to Endon Quarry. Before the gate, turn right up a narrow path (signposted) which then curves left to climb up the hillside by cottages. Be careful, for the workings are very dangerous. They must have looked very barren before the scars of old workings began to grow over and tree cover improved the site.

Kerridge Ridge

Cross a stile half way up and then proceed ahead to cross two stiles at the top of Kerridge Ridge. The view across to Rainow and western Peakland is impressive. Do not turn right or left but keep ahead on a wide green path, which soon begins to wind gently to the right by hawthorns. Be vigilant here, for your way is the less distinct and steep path heading down the hillside from this green swathe. It is hard to believe that this side of the hill was mined for coal and that the valley below housed several early mills. Nature heals very quickly. Head for the solitary hawthorn mid-field and a more obvious cross-path. The River Dean can be seen below. Beyond is Hough Hole House, where there is a Victorian allegorical garden based on the opening to the "Pilgrim's Progress" story. The garden, known as Mellors Garden after its creator James Mellor, is open to the public on limited occasions.

Turn left and walk to the field boundary where a stone step-stile is crossed. The path rises gently left by a tree belt, sheltering a house to the right. Go through a gate and follow the path across the field, with stone slabs on the ground in places. Pass through the stone gateway and take the right fork above a wood, the path leading to a wooden gate. Go through it and descend to pass by a cottage. The cascade of water to the right is where the Dean was damned to produce a head of water for the mills in the valley.

Continue ahead as the road descends towards the mills. Very shortly, look for a stile on the right (on the Gritstone Trail) which is crossed. This leads over a bridge and curves left to climb up the valley side to a gap-stile and up steps to another. There's a beautiful little dell to the left, sadly marred by dumping. Keep ahead and cross a stile by converted buildings at this one time private college. Walk a short distance to a wooden stile. Cross this and turn left to cross a stone stile.

Oakenbank

The path proceeds to a cross a stile by a farm on the right. It then keeps company with a wall on the left as it descends steps to a bridge and up to a metalled road. Keep ahead along Oakenbank Lane to Blaze Hill. Turn left here and walk down the road as it bears left into Bollington, passing The Poachers Inn and on to the Turners Arms (Returning point for bus travellers). At the junction keep ahead, to walk along Bollington's main street. By the traffic lights, it curves to go under the aqueduct. You can cut through the park on the right, where bowls and cricket are often played, back to the Adlington Road and The Vale Inn.

Walk 15: Combs

The Route: Rye Flatt farm, Combs, Combs reservoir, Combs golf course, Down Lee Farm

Distance: 8 km (5 mls)

Map: Ordnance Survey Leisure Series 24 – The Peak District, White Peak Area

How to get there:

By Train – Chapel-en-le-Frith railway station (start point) is served daily by trains from Buxton or Manchester.

By Car – Travel on the A6 to the Chapel-en-le-Frith by pass, turn into the town then follow the signs to Chapel-en-le-Frith railway station.

The Beehive at Combs is a friendly local, standing in the heart of this quiet hamlet. It has a small bar and large lounge, both of which are comfortable and welcoming. The bar used to be called the Hikers' Bar. The Beehive is open from noon until 3pm and from 7 pm onwards on Mondays to Saturdays and usual hours on Sundays. Marstons Pedigree and Tetleys bitter are on draught and food is also on offer.

In 1864 the building was extended from an original cottage on what was the village green. It is remarkable that the pub has survived, given the isolated position of the hamlet, tucked away between the railway line and the impenetrable Combs Moss. It is an ideal calling point mid-way on this ramble.

The Walk

Start at Chapel-en-le-Frith railway station, which looks almost continental to match the name. The station building is now a restaurant and passengers purchase tickets for the train from a machine or the guard. The station was the scene of a runaway freight train accident some years back. Thanks to the gallant driver, John Axon, the collision was minimised, but he lost his life. His deed is immortalised in the Ballad of John Axon. From the north western end of the platform, in the direction of Manchester, leave from the station building side and go through a kissing-gate down to a track. Bear left under the railway bridge and then go right, up steps in the wall. The path climbs to the right, through woodland to a drive. Woodpeckers can often be heard here. Just before the drive cross a stile on the right over a wall.

View of Goyt

Keep ahead along the bank on a well worn path, moving away from the wall and almost parallel with the drive above. The view of Combs reservoir and the Goyt is delicious on a summers evening here, when a thin cloud cover creams around Eccles pike as the sun goes down. You come to a cross path, but keep ahead and climb to a stile close to the top left corner. Go ahead to a gap in the next wall. Once through, head right – but not to the far right corner. You will see two gateways. Choose the one on the right and proceed down the hill towards Rye Flatt Farm keeping close to the wall on your left. This brings you to the edge of a stream and by an old mill pond. The clear path leads down to the road. Bear right and walk into the hamlet of Combs.

The Beehive

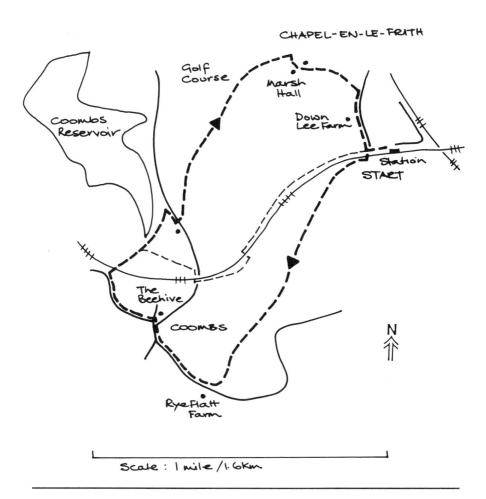

CHAPEL-EN-LE-FRITH

Golf Course

Marsh Hall

Coombs Reservoir

Down Lee Farm

Station
START

The Beehive

COOMBS

N

Rye Flatt Farm

Scale : 1 mile / 1.6km

Invention

The route comes right to the Beehive pub. Combs was where Bert Froode invented the brake shoe, having observed the efforts of farmers to slow down using other means such as their own boots. He began to create the famous Ferodo company from this small start – a little-known fact is that Ferodo is an anagram of Bert's surname. Otherwise, not much has changed, for the gritstone edges hemming in this community are still lined with farms eking out a living by rearing sheep for market.

Bear left at the pub to walk along a lane, (but do not go immediately right), by a new post office and into countryside again. As the road bends sharp left before the railway, go right, through a gap-stile, as signposted, and walk under the railway bridge. Go almost immediately right afterwards over a stile and along a green path leading to a footbridge and then left to cross another. Those wishing to take a short cut should go right at this point, through a gateway, heading to the right of a barn. On the road go right and at the other side of the underbridge bear left up a well trodden path leading back to Chapel station.

Combs reservoir

Otherwise, those choosing the longer route should keep ahead through wet ground at the head of the reservoir. The path climbs up towards a fence and behind a bungalow. Do not go through the gate but, as waymarked, go between holly bushes, over a footbridge and cross a stile leading onto a road.

Go right for a short section and, opposite the bungalow, go left over a stile to follow the hedge on your right through a wet patch. Go through a gap by a hedge leading off left. Then go through the next gateway on the right. Once through head very slightly left, almost diagonally across the field and keep to the right of an electricity pole. Walk across the small enclosure, bearing left to a short wet track and a stile. Cross it.

The path follows the right-hand hedge to cross another stile and footbridge and keeps ahead along a slight indent, which presumably is the base of a grubbed up hedge. Cross a stile into the golf course again and go over the footbridge. Then bear right to a stile near to the field corner. Once over, keep straight on, with a hedge to the left and continue to a stile leading to a drive.

Down Lee Farm

Go right here on a track to pass between superbly restored buildings to a small gate ahead. This leads into an old pasture, often wet on the ground, where you bear left to cross a stile. Then, keep ahead with a hedge to the left through a long field. Cross a stile and narrow enclosure to exit at a kissing gate onto a road. Go right and pass Down Lee Farm and go up to the railway. Bear left before the railway line to retrace steps to Chapel station.

Walk 16: Chapel-en-le-Frith

The Route: Burrfields, Bowden Hall, Wash, Shireoaks, Breckhead, Breckend, Chapel Milton, Bridgeholm Green, The Courses

Distance: 8 km (5 mls)

Start: The Market Place, Chapel-en-le-Frith. (Grid Reference 057808)

Map: Ordnance Survey Outdoor Leisure 1 – The Peak District, Dark Peak Area

How to get there:

By Bus – There is a regular daily service from Manchester, Buxton, Derby and Nottingham. A less frequent service operates from Chesterfield

By Car – Travel on the A6 between Buxton and Manchester. Chapel-en-le-Frith is signposted from the by-pass.

Derbyshire Ale, CAMRA's guide to drinking in these parts comments on The Royal Oak:

"An unexceptional facade conceals a hotel of exceptional character". This could not be more true for this sixteenth century coaching inn was once used as a magistrates' court and many a rogue has been sentenced within these walls.

The Royal Oak pub is open from noon to 3 pm and from 7 pm onwards on Mondays to Saturdays. Usual opening on Sundays. Food is generally not served but bed and breakfast accommodation is available. The draught beers on offer are Tetleys Dark Mild and Tetleys Bitter. The Royal Oak is surrounded by pubs, so try The Roebuck opposite (Tetleys) or The Jolly Carter (Robinsons) on the edge of town towards Buxton, if you happen to be exceptionally thirsty.

The Walk

Start from the water trough in the Market Place, next to the old market cross and nearby stocks. Such features would have been commonplace even in the last century. Surprisingly few have survived the motor car era. Bear right to walk along the Market Place and, at the corner with Church Brow (note the bull on the house opposite), continue ahead choosing the right of the two narrow tarmac lanes.

The Parish Church, Chapel-en-le-Frith

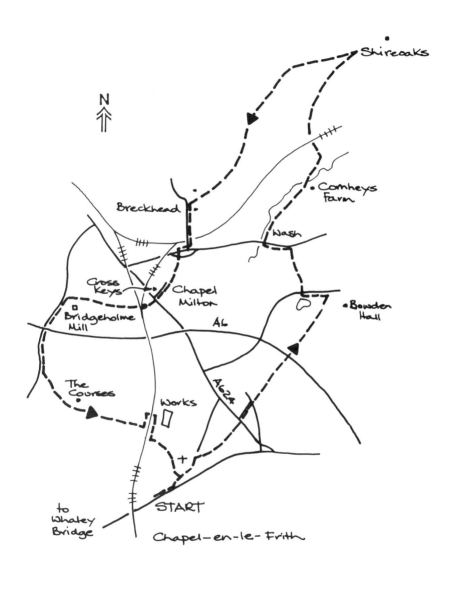

Scale: 1 mile/1.6 km

Black Hole

Chapel-en-le-Frith church looks impressive through the stone gate posts, in a commanding position above the town. Perhaps, this is why the Roundheads during the Civil War decided to incarcerate as many as 1500 Scottish Royalists in the building. On their release, forty-four were found dead and many more barely alive. Since then the church has been known as Derbyshires Black Hole.

The lane begins to curve left and at this point look for a path leading off right between a hedge and wire fence to an estate road. Cross this and then bear left to walk down another path behind houses, to a bridge across a stream. Then, go ahead to a kissing gate and the main A624. Cross over and enter a road known as The Crescent. As this curves away to the left, keep ahead between houses on a path signposted to Bowden.

Proceed down steps and cross a narrow lane, and then up steps by a tall Victorian dwelling. Keep ahead, passing by a factory into open countryside with a view on the left across to Chinley Churn and Mount Famine. This was named because cattle or sheep never thrived on its pastures.

The path soon comes to the main by-pass road which, despite the roar of traffic, is never really busy, but you still have to be vigilant when crossing. Fortunately, traffic tends to be slowing for the nearby roundabout. On the other side, walk down steps and keep ahead. Pass between a pool on the left and Bowden Hall on the right, seen through a plantation of slender beech trees. The path exits by a white gate onto a road.

Turn left and after two metres go right by the signpost to cross a trickle of a stream to reach a stone step-stile. Cross this and then head left to cut across the field to another stone step-stile. Once over, follow the path as it continues very slightly left to pass an old barn and through a gap in a broken-down wall. The path keeps company with a line of thorns and holly on the left and then drops to a back lane.

Slab Bridge

Go left here by the few houses which comprise the hamlet of Wash. The road steepens and falls to a bridge. Do not cross this, but go right at the signpost into rough pasture. Continue ahead, with the stream to the left and Cornheys comes into view. Go through wet ground and then edge closer to the brook. Cross the fine stone-slab bridge on the left and then turn right to cross a drive. Go over a stile, which sometimes has a warning about bulls – not that we have ever seen one in this field. Look before entering and, if all clear, head away from the stream to climb the small bluff and exit by way of a gate in the field corner.

Another World

Once on the road look for a gap-stile on the other side and walk towards the horseshoe shape of the railway underbridge. It is like stepping into another world on the other side, the landscape being wilder and more windswept – even the noise of the A6 is dampened. The path follows the wall and is soon waymarked left to a stile by a holly tree. Once over, head very slightly right up the field bank to the top left corner, where two fine stone gateposts still stand.

Continue ahead beneath hawthorn boughs on what was an old track. Follow this to just before the isolated farmstead of Shireoaks. You approach a gateway and ruins of an old barn on the right, where you turn left along an aggregate track. Climb gently up through the field and head back towards Chapel. The views across to the town and the brooding Combs Moss beyond are fascinating. The two chimneys of the Ferodo works and the church tower are a landmark now for most of the walk back.

Breckhead

Once through the next gateway take the left fork and the way is now straightforward, until the cluster of houses at Breckhead. Simply, follow the track past the old hut and through a succession of gates as it descends gently to the few houses of Breckhead. The track curves left here and then right to reach a metalled road. Turn left and walk down to cross the railway bridge and at the junction bear right. This little stretch soon leads to a lower junction. Bear left on the lower road, signposted to Wash. Within a few paces cross the road and go through a squeeze stile. Follow the embankment and exit into a small enclosure where the path cuts across to a white house and a lane. Turn right and follow this down to the Cross Keys public house at Chapel Milton. This sells draught Thwaites and has been altered to accommodate a small restaurant.

Double Viaduct

The impressive double viaduct of the quarry line to Buxton stands above you – often a train sits on one of these arms waiting for clearance to enter the main line. Cross the road and turn left but within a few paces bear right as signposted, along a path beneath the great arches. Climb over a ladder stile – the path leads to the right, near to the stream, and soon approaches an old mill complex which now houses a number of small works. Cross the step-stile by a gate and walk ahead through the yard.

The old Bridgeholme Mill on the right is a sorry sight. Hopefully, it will be refurbished in the near future. Turn left and walk up the road which passes under the by pass and climbs past a farm. Shortly, look for a track leading off left. Cross a stile by a gate and go straight on along the green lane. Cross a stile into a field and use the stones to tip toe over the stream. The old track is still discernible in the field as it climbs to a stile on the right. Cross this and turn left to climb the bank, passing by a farm and houses known as The Crosses. Cross a stile by the old bath and proceed ahead by the Victorian lamp post. The path keeps to the right of the garden hedge and crosses a makeshift stile into a field.

The path now rises to a brow and the view of the two chimneys returns. Cross a stile and drop down the side of the field to a track below. Go left and then right under the railway and right along the path as it skirts allotments and then dips down left by the works. The path rises by the churchyard and passes between houses to exit on Church Brow. Turn right, back to the Market Place.

Walk 17: Whaley Bridge

The Route: Horwich End, Taxal Church, Taxal Moor, Clayton Fold Farm, Kettleshulme, Kishfield Lane, Slaters Bank Wood, Todd Brook Reservoir

Distance: 10 km (6 mls)

Start: Whaley Bridge Railway station (Grid Reference 012815)

Maps: Ordnance Survey Outdoor Leisure 1 The Peak District; Dark Peak Area, Outdoor Leisure 24 The Peak District; White Peak Area, and Pathfinder Sheet Stockport (South)

How to get there:

By Bus and Train – Whaley Bridge is very well served daily by bus and train from Manchester and Buxton. There is a limited service from Macclesfield.

By Car – Whaley Bridge is signposted off the A6 by pass. There is car parking down Canal Street beyond the old canal transhipment shed.

Be warned, the walk through Whaley Bridge offers temptation. The rambler must have a strong constitution to walk by so many public houses. Start from Whaley Bridge railway station to pass by The Jodrell Arms to the main street. Cross the road by The Station public house, serving a lovely pint of Robinsons. Turn right to walk along the street to pass shops, the White Hart public house, a fish and chip shop and then come to the Shepherd's Arms Inn on the left.

This delightful pub serves Marstons Mercian mild, Burton Bitter and Pedigree and is essential for the person who enjoys old pubs. It was built in the early 1600s as a farmhouse and the original stone-flagged floor remains in the tap room. The temptation to resist a juke box and other machines is a tribute to the landlord and landlady's determination to offer "just good ale and company".

The Shepherd's Arms Inn is open from 11.30 am until 3 pm and from 7pm onwards on Mondays to Saturdays. Sundays usual hours. Food is not served and there is a garden area which is well used on warmer days. This is a pub not to be missed.

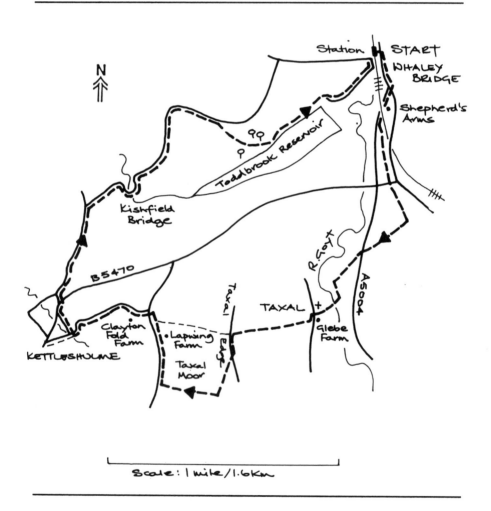

Scale: 1 mile/1.6 Km

The Walk

Retrace your steps to the road and turn left to go under the railway bridge. After the Cock Inn, look for a little path on the left which leads up to the old trackbed of the Cromford and High Peak railway. Go right.

Cromford and High Peak Railway

The railway, built in the 1830s to link the Peak Forest and Cromford Canals, was a most unusual affair. It was built by a canal engineer and it shows. The last section closed in 1967 and much of the line is now part of the High Peak Trail. It is a great pity that other sections are not converted to such use between Buxton and Whaley Bridge.

The old railway line comes to a road, New Cross Road, just beyond Cromford Court. Bear right for a short distance and look for a path leading off right, through a childrens play area and into Mevril Road. Continue ahead to the main road. Cross this and keep ahead to pass by bungalows to a small gate by a large gate.

Michael Heathcote

Continue along the track down to the footbridge which is crossed. The path then climbs by the lovely old church and churchyard of Taxal, a peaceful haven in this secluded part of the Goyt valley. There is a memorial in the churchyard to Michael Heathcote, "Gentleman of the pantry and yeoman of the mouth to his late Majesty King George the Second". Mr Heathcote lived from the late 16th century until 1763, reaching an age of 73, which is remarkable considering the risks a food taster takes for any monarch.

At the metalled road, turn left. Opposite Glebe Farm, go right, over a step-stile by a gate, the way being signposted to Taxal Edge by another fine Derbyshire open-air bath! Cross the stile in the next field boundary and keep ahead to cross two further gap-stiles. Proceed in a similar direction to cross another stile before ploughing on to a ladder stile, which is also crossed.

Taxal Edge

There is a path on the opposite side of the road through the woodland over Taxal Moor. It descends straight ahead through two fields to a point on the road above Kettleshulme. A far more dramatic route, however, is to bear left. At the edge of the wooded area, look for a well-worn path leading off right, up the hillside through patches of rhododendrons. This soon becomes a classic green sunken way, curving upwards to breach Taxal Edge with splendid views across to Charles Head and beyond.

The path leads to a wooden ladder stile and once over heads right, through rough ground to exit onto a road.

Go right and walk past Lapwing Farm. As the road dips down by another house, turn left down a lesser road to pass Clayton Fold Farm, no doubt with dogs barking and geese hissing. The lane narrows and becomes more of a track down to Kettleshulme village.

At the junction by the bridge, bear left and follow this around to The Bull's Head in Kettleshulme, a good local hostelry featured in Pub Walks in Cheshire. It is not usually open at lunchtimes, on Mondays-Fridays. Opposite is the Tea Cosy cafe. After the refreshment stop, cross the road and bear right to pass a garden centre on the left and at the next corner bear left down Kishfield Lane.

Lumbhole Mill

Follow this lane into the valley. There is a view of the old Lumbhole Mill – a cotton mill dating from the latter part of the eighteenth century. In the nineteenth century, candlewicks for miners lamps were made here. Not far along the road forks. Bear right and descend to Kishfield Bridge, a most secluded spot. The road is paved with setts and climbs up the bank by the cottages.

At the top, the road bends right and begins to descend gradually between houses. Be vigilant here – after Croft Cottage, look for a path on the right between a fence and wall down to a gate. The path then curves left between trees and behind gardens to a lovely seat to rest awhile. Continue to a stile leading into Slaterbank Wood above Todd Brook reservoir. Take the lower level path to the left, weaving between rhododendrons before reaching a road. Go left here and follow this road down to Whaley Bridge railway station.

· The terminus of the Peak Forest Canal, Whaley Bridge

Walk 18: Bradwell

The Route: Grey Ditch, Bothams Farm, Rebellion Knoll, Robin Hood's Cross, Bradwell Edge

Distance: 5 km (3 mls)

Start: Public Toilets, Bradwell (Grid Reference 174811)

Map: Ordnance Survey Outdoor Leisure No. 1 The Peak District; Dark Peak Area

How to get there:

By Bus – There is a regular daily service from Sheffield and summer Sunday services from other parts of the Peak District

By Car – From Sheffield travel on the A625 into the Hope Valley and then the B6049. From the west travel on the A623 to Tideswell Cross Roads and then bear left onto the B6049. There is limited on street parking in the village.

The Valley Lodge, which used to be known as The Shoulder of Mutton, is a modern looking pub in the centre of Bradwell. It opens from noon until 4 pm Monday to Saturday and usually from 7 pm in the evenings. Usual Sunday hours. The pub has several bars serving draught beers from Stones, Wards and Youngers. Sometimes other guest beers are available. Meals are always available when the pub is open and there is a small drinking area outside. Please note that there is a definite rule about ramblers not eating their own food here.

Those who like to sit and watch birds (the feathered variety) do not need to wipe their glasses if they think they see colourful sparrows here. It is not unusual to spot budgies flying between the roofs of surrounding houses!

Two other pubs worth of note in the village are The White Hart, a few minutes walk away in Town Gate and The Old Bowling Green up in Smalldale.

Bradwell still has the feel of being more of a working village than a dormitory centre. The cabinet maker, builder's merchant and ice cream producer have all survived and there's a busy feel about the village which has not been lost since its mining days. The village was well-known for its production of a very hard hat for miners referred to as a "Bradder Beaver". People sometimes still refer to Bradwell as "Bradder". Bagshawe Cavern is open to the public, but it is not an easy underground journey like the show caves in nearby Castleton. It is entered by one of the old mine workings.

The Walk

Start from the public toilets by the village green. Turn right to walk to the main road. Cross over, go right, across the bridge and first left along Soft Water Lane, referring to the Bradwell Brook on the left. Pass the Royal British Legion building and go through a gap-stile to the right. Walk through a small enclosure and another gap-stile. Proceed ahead on the well-worn path to the right of a barn to another gap-stile. Go ahead to yet another stile by a recently rebuilt house on the left.

Grey Ditch

At the next straggled hedge, cut off right, up the field to a gap-stile in the next hedge. Continue to climb in a similar direction, crossing the slight remains of a curious indent known as Grey Ditch, to a wooden stile just beyond. Go through a wet patch and keep company with the hedge to the left, to a stile by a water trough. Cross it and walk up the track. The map shows a slight variation to this, but most locals simply follow the track towards Bothams Farm.

Just before the entrance there is a stile on the right. Cross this and follow the field's edge on the left above the buildings. The path dips to a stile by a gate then bears right, curving up the bank. Views over to Castleton are impressive, despite the cement works. Continue to contour along the hillside – first above scrub and then through it, to a stone gap-stile. The barred gate seen clearly to the right is not the way! Once through the stile join a track.

Overdale

Bear right to climb above Overdale with views across to Shatton Moor. The track rises, curves left and levels out. As you approach a gate, bear right to go over a stone step-stile. Continue ahead by a point known as Robin Hood's Cross, another reference to that mythical character who has bequeathed a thousand legends to the land. Go through a gap-stile and ahead again to another.

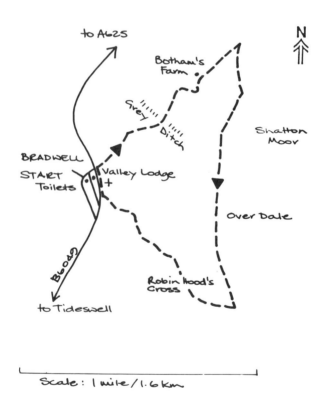

You now begin to drop more precipitously towards the village of Bradwell, a settlement known to the Romans, being on their Batham Road. The church stands at the centre of the village – a large structure restored considerably over the past two hundred years.

The path curves down to cross the remnants of a dry stone wall. It then zig-zags down to a wicket gate and stile

Bradwell Church

leading to a track. Walk down it to pass a secluded house on the right. At the corner beyond, keep ahead along a lesser green lane. At the next junction go left and then drop down to pass a house and bear right into the village as the road twists between old cottages. The thoroughfare, Bessie Lane, leads to steps down past an old post box, to the main road and Valley Lodge.

Walk 19: Chinley

The Route: Whitehough, Eccles Fold, Buxworth, Brierley Green, Stubbins

Distance: 6 km (4 mls)

Start: Chinley Railway station (Grid Reference 038827

Map: Outdoor Leisure No. 1 The Peak District, Dark Peak Area

How to get there:

By Bus and Train – There is a daily train service from Sheffield and Manchester. There is also a Monday-Saturday bus service from Buxton.

By Car – From the east, travel on the A6 from Buxton to Chapel-en-le-Frith and then the A624 and B6062. From the west, travel on the A6 to Bridgemont and then turn left onto the B6062. This turn is very awkward and is best approached by going to the main roundabout at Whaley Bridge and doubling back for a right turn at Bridgemont. There is limited on street parking in the village of Chinley.

The Oddfellows Arms, in the quiet backwater of Whitehough, is a resilient old pub having resisted nearby competition at The Old Hall (no longer a pub) for years. The Oddfellows serves Marstons Best and Pedigree in a homely bar between noon and 3 pm and from 7 pm in the evenings. Food is generally not available. This friendly local is well worth a visit.

The Walk

Start the walk from Chinley Station, at one time a place of importance where people transferred from one train to another. In recent years, the characteristic station buildings have been dismantled and railway tracks "rationalised", making it a cold place. Leave from the station entrance and turn left along Station Road to Squirrel Green, the large pub opposite being the old Railway Hotel. It is a local popular haunt which welcomes ramblers.

Cross the road and bear right to pass by the green. At the corner, as the road bends right, continue ahead in the direction of Whitehough. The road crosses the old Peak Forest Tram Road, which ran from a transhipment centre with the canal at Buxworth to Dove Holes (near Buxton). Carry on along the road which soon rises into the hamlet of Whitehough.

The Oddfellows Arms

The Oddfellows Arms stands on the left and a road leads off right by a well. Continue to climb the bank on the "main" road.

Go over the A6 and then turn next right along Eccles Terrace. At the end of this road go left through a gap-stile by a gate and walk up the drive. As this bends right continue ahead along a swathe of grass to cross a stile into a field. Proceed ahead along a well-worn path to cross a stone stile into a lane.

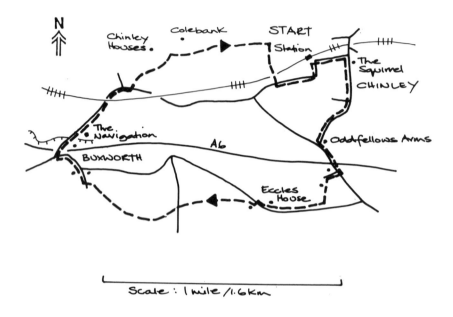

Eccles House

Bear right and pass by the pretentious gateway to Eccles House. The road by passes the house and comes to a small group of cottages and a farm, known as Eccles Fold. The road twists right and then left. At this point bear left up a tarmac drive with restored cottages to the left and a barn on the right. Thankfully, the tarmac stops after a few metres and you leave Eccles Fold by way of a gate onto a superb green lane, offering views across to Chinley Churn and Cracken Edge.

Follow this until it exits at a stone step-stile onto a triangular patch of land covered in gorse. There is a good view of Buxworth below. Take the right fork down to the road and opposite is a stone step-stile. Cross it and enter a field. Bear left down the field, and cross the remains of a dry stone wall before reaching the intact wall on the left just beyond. Follow this down the hill to wet ground. Before the stream bear right to cut across to a stile. Cross this and, in the next field, bear right. Go ahead towards a point where the dry stone wall looks as if it is meeting the end gable of a house.

Buxworth

The path climbs up the bank to pass behind cottages to a rusty barred gate on the right. Go through this and walk down the track to a road. Turn left here and soon another road is reached. Go right to cross again and then proceed along the A6 road, unless diverting to walk around the restored inland dock of Buxworth. This short branch of the Peak Forest Canal was at one time a busy transhipment centre for agricultural goods, coal and lime coming down the Peak Forest Tramway. There would have been dozens of narrow boats unloading in these wharfs. Thanks to the Inland Waterways Association and other organisations, the complex is slowly coming back to life again.

Petition

On the right stands the Navigation public house, obviously named in honour of the canal, which serves draught beers and offers a welcome to ramblers. Buxworth is an unusual name and is derived from a medieval bailiff of the Royal Forest, Ralph Bugge. Originally, the village name was 'Bugsworth' and caused considerable consternation to the residents including the local vicar, who led the petitioning of Parliament for a change of name. Parliament was sympathetic and Punch magazine, a sad recent loss after 150 years, ran a campaign on the story. Despite the change, the story still brings a smile to those in the know.

The road rises to a junction by the school and opposite stands the old Bull's Head. It looks as if it should still be a wayside inn! To the right, in the valley, runs the line of the old tramroad. At the junction cross the road and bear right to walk up the bank and under the railway bridge to Brierley Green. Pass Dolly Lane and a few metres beyond, before the road sign go left up a track leading to an open green at the back of the houses. Keep ahead to cross a stile by a gate and continue to climb up the green way which can become very wet in winter. This gives out into a field below Chinley Houses Farm. Ahead by the bank of trees is Cotebank. Your way is to follow the dry stone wall to the right as it curves around to join another green track leading to a gap-stile by a gate.

Tracks

There is a choice of tracks here, to the left, right or ahead. Keep ahead, with Cotebank to the left up the bank. The track soon with an aggregate base, passes cottages and farms. Pass by several old farm buildings and, opposite a well, go right, through a gap-stile onto a small green (if you reach a tarmac lane you have gone too far). Walk down the gentle bank to meet a more prominent path coming in from the right. Keep ahead and the path soon descends to a footbridge over the Manchester to Sheffield railway line. Once on Station Road, turn left for the short walk into Chinley.

The Memorial at Chinley, one of many in the Peak District

Walk 20: Padley Gorge from Hathersage

The Route: Longshaw estate car park, Padley Gorge, Grindleford, Leadmill Bridge, Hathersage, North Lees, Stanage Edge, Burbage Rocks

Distance: 18 km (11 mls)

Start: Longshaw Car Park (National Trust) at Grid Reference 267802. Public transport users should alight at Fox House

Maps: Ordnance Survey Leisure No 24 – The Peak District, White Peak Area and Pathfinder sheet 743, Sheffield

How to get there:

By Bus – There is a good daily service from Sheffield, Castleton and Bakewell. There is a seasonal service from Chesterfield and Dronfield.

By Car – Travel on the A625 to Fox House then on the B6055. The car park is signposted (not very well) about 200 yards from the junction. Alternatively, travel on the B6054 from Owler Bar to Wooden Pole (B6055/6054 junction). Follow the B6055 past the B6450 turning. The car park is signposted on the left.

The Plough at Leadmill Bridge opens 11.30 am until 3 pm on Monday to Saturday and from 5.30 pm in the evening. It serves Tetleys Bitter and both snack and full meals. Previously a farmhouse, this welcoming pub with a large lounge and smaller tap room is used to walkers calling for refreshment.

The Plough offers good views to the surrounding heights from the Derwent Valley and is justifiably popular with locals and visitors.

The Walk

Start the walk by taking the path out of Longshaw rear of the car park and follow the route right, to the Longshaw Lodge Gate. (If coming from the Fox House bus stop, walk to the B6055 junction and go through a gate on the far side of the A625. The path leads down to the white gate of Longshaw Lodge.) Go through the gate, cross the road and over the stile opposite, by another white gate. All of this land belongs to the National Trust's Longshawe Estate and is well-used because of its proximity to Sheffield.

The Plough

Padley Gorge

The path is easily followed through the wood, with views left to Sir William Hill with its TV mast and to the contorted stones of Mother Cap, perched on Millstone Edge. At the fork in the path keep left, descend to a footbridge over the Burbage Brook. Cross the bridge and bear left along a path near to the stream.

Do not follow the broad path which veers away from the stream or go over the footbridge to the left. Instead, continue ahead alongside the stream and enter the oak woods of Padley Gorge. This superb wood is a wonderful survival of the ancient woodland which once dominated the valleys of the Peak District. Its continuation is now a result of careful management, not least being the restriction on the grazing of sheep. For

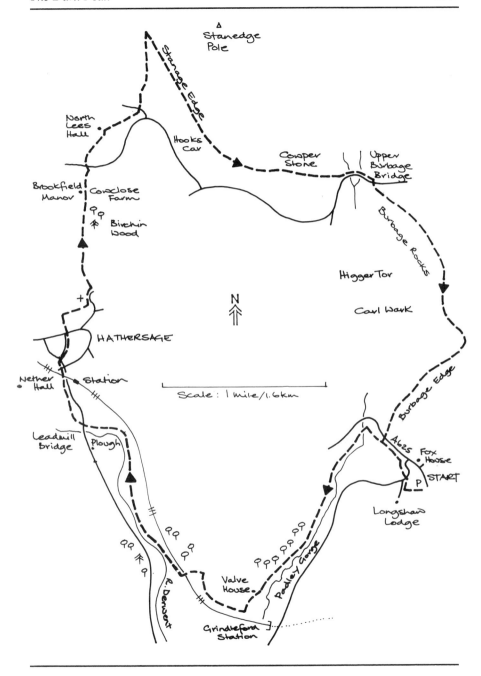

a long time the moorland sheep wintered in the wood, effectively removing any newly seeded young trees. This practice has now ceased and the new growth of both trees and other flora is startling.

The path falls steadily, but the stream descends more rapidly and soon the path is high above the incisive brook. Ignore paths leading up the hill or down to the stream. Keep on past a ruined building on the right, before reaching a curved roof valve house on the great Derwent Aqueduct, built in the early part of the century. This carries water from the Derwent Dams, down the valley to Derby and the East Midlands.

Valve House

Bear left by the valve house, following a path down to the gate. You come into a rough lane between the houses of Windses Estate. At the bottom of the lane there is a T-junction. To the left is Grindleford station (trains to Sheffield and Manchester) and a cafe. Go right at the T-junction, along a lane, soon leaving the houses behind and passing Padley Manor Farm. The track continues and soon reaches Padley Chapel. This is a reminder of the persecution of local Catholics in earlier times and the centre of an annual pilgrimage to this day. On the left is Brunts Barn, the Peak Park's volunteer centre, dedicated to the late Harry Brunt. For a long time, Harry was the Deputy National Park Officer of the Peak Park.

Continue on the track over the cattle grid and the remains of a bridge. This once carried the route over a deep cutting which was dug for the Derwent Water Boards railway. The line was built to carry building stone from Bolehill Quarry to the Midland Railway at Grindleford. From there, it went on to Bamford and the Derwent and Howden dam sites.

Carry on, past the houses on the left, and go through a gateway. Bear left here, leaving the track and follow a scanty path by the edge of the bracken and woodland. This path soon joins another and bears left, down through the wood to a ladder stile by the railway bridge. Once over the bridge, go right, through a gate into Coppice Wood. The path is now easily followed but is rough underfoot. At the bottom of the hill, the riverside path is joined. Turn right here and soon gain open fields near to the River Derwent.

There follows a delightful riverside walk, but after the second stile the path cuts off a loop of the river by bearing right to Harper Lees. Waymarks point round the buildings to a kissing gate and lane then rejoining the riverside. Notice the collection of odd carved stones here. It looks as if someone had the idea of building a mock Grecian temple, collected stones and then thought better of the project.

Kingfishers

Continue along the lane, or along the immediately adjacent river bank. There are often dippers, wagtails and kingfishers hereabouts. The lane soon runs alongside a mill leat, still carrying water and heralding the approach to Leadmill Bridge. At the main road turn left to go over the bridge and up to The Plough public house.

Retrace your steps from the pub over the bridge, then look for a stile on the left which is crossed. Head across the field to the roadside hedge, just to the left of the road sign. Here you will find a stile leading onto the road again. Looking left, you can see the tower and flag pole of Nether Hall. Turn left along the road and go under the railway bridge. Take care as there is no footway. Once past station approach, cross the road and continue along the main Hathersage Road to Oddfellows Road, which is signposted to a car park and swimming baths.

As you walk along Oddfellows Road, Stanage Edge can be seen away to the left, rising above the roofs of Hathersage. Continue beyond the car park. At a green lamp post, where the road swings right, go straight on along a signposted footpath. Pass between farm buildings to the main road, emerging opposite the Hathersage Inn.

Little John

Cross the road and proceed along Baulk Lane ahead. Look for a signpost on the right which points the way to the church, via the wet weather route. The church spire can be seen ahead and Stanage Edge to the left. Follow the clear path to the church and enter the churchyard. The church is dedicated to St Michael and All Angels and the churchyard contains the supposed grave of Little John, Robin Hood's giant lieutenant. It is said that a large yew bow hung in the church until the 19th century, but this has mysteriously vanished. Robin Hood has been the subject of folklore in these parts for decades. It was not long ago that

Sheffield laid claim to the home ground of Robin Hood of Loxley (i.e. Loxley near Sheffield) rather than Nottinghamshire's Sherwood Forest. At the time this caused something of a stir though Nottingham has perhaps won the day. Who knows, more vital evidence might emerge.

Little John's Grave

Ancient Cross

Go through the churchyard, by the stump of an ancient cross and out via the lych gate. These covered gateways were designed to allow coffin bearers to rest before the final walk to the church.

Turn left along a lane to a stile and a green lane. Go right. The path splits three ways. The right and straight-on routes are clear but you take the left-hand way by an ash tree. This is steep and has a few steps into the field. The path then goes straight down to a stone clapper bridge over a muddy trickle.

From the bridge go straight on, with fence and hedge to the left. At the top of the rise there is a fence at right angles to the line of march and in its centre is a stile. This is your route. Once over the stile continue up the hill to join an old lane near a rickety gate. This was obviously a cart road from Hathersage at one time. It ran down to the stream at an easier gradient than the path you have just used, turned a hairpin bend and climbed up to meet the path again. It has gone out of use now but it is fascinating to sort out these old pieces of trackway and conjecture on their uses. Go left through the gate. The "lane" appears as no more than a terrace on the hillside with an overgrown hedge to the left and Birchill wood away on the right. Brookfield Manor, now a conference centre, can be seen below to the left and Cowclose farm ahead with North Less hall and Stanage Edge beyond.

North Lees Hall

When you reach Cowclose Farm, go through the gate but do not go through the farmyard. Instead, skirt to the right of the barn, then to the left to a little wooden gate before regaining the track again. Continue along the farm track to the road and here go left, then almost at once right, up the driveway to North Lees Hall. This hall is known for its association with Charlotte Bronte as the setting for Thornfield Hall in the novel "Jane Eyre". The hall has its own fascinating history. It was one of the properties built by the Eyre family, noted catholics at a time when such religious faith was tantamount to treason. A ruined chapel close by the hall was built at the time of James II, whose leanings to Catholicism cost him his throne. Such anti-Catholic feeling also led to the sacking of the chapel.

Skirt the hall, now a series of holiday flats, and go right, up the steps as signed, to a gateway into open fields. The path is signposted straight on, not right towards the obvious gate. Go across the field to a stile by another gate and enter a wood. The path through the wood is a broad track which should be followed until just before it reaches the road. Then a rough but clear path climbs away to the left, to emerge by the Ranger Briefing Centre and toilets.

Stanage Edge

Cross the road and head up the broad green path opposite with the climbing edges of Stanage now close ahead and seemingly impregnable. The view from this path is extensive, to Offerton Hill and round to Mam Tor. This path soon becomes paved and passes through a gate into a wood, then rises steadily through a jumble of boulders with the climbing edges to the right. Ignore various paths going right. These are climbers' paths and should not be followed. The path continues through a sheepfold and ascends a weakness in the gritstone face, swings right and the crest of Stanage Edge is achieved.

There follows a superb walk along this, one of the most spectacular climbing edges of the Peak. The views are breathtaking and take in most of The High Peak-Win Hill, Kinder Scout and Bleaklow. To the left is Stanage Pole which marks the route of the Long Causeway, an ancient route from the Hope Valley to Sheffield. Keep on the edge path, which is completely clear underfoot. Beyond Hooks Car, the path turns more to the east. The main path avoids the trig point and another path descends to the road. Take neither, but use the narrow track to the trig point for another brilliant view. Retrace your steps back to the main path and then go right. Descend by Cowper Stone and over the moor to Upper Burbage Bridge, where often there is an ice cream van during the summer.

Cross the two bridges and then take the second stile on the right, ignoring the more obvious lower path. There is no sign at this second stile. The path is clear enough, though narrow, along the top of Burbage Rocks. Again, the view is superb, taking in Carl Wark, an old hillfort site, and Higger Tor.

Eventually, the path tends downward, through tumbled boulders and then swings left to join another path by a ruined wall. Some of the wall has been used to make cairns and, at the second of these, there is a crossing of paths. Go straight on but easing right as you climb again to the crest of the rocks. There are some dramatic rock faces on this stretch, the work of early quarrymen. At the biggest quarry there are a number of millstones in various stages of "construction", left when the quarry closed. The overhangs here are spectacular and the edges loose, so keep away.

Ahead can be seen Longshaw Pond and the main road heading to Surprise View. The path descends now, past an abandoned part-hollowed out stone trough, to join a lower path and then the A625 road at a stile. Rather than finish this walk on the road, cross over and go through the stile opposite into Longshaw Estate again. You soon join your outward route and bear left, retracing your steps, past the two white gates to the car park or bus stop. Longshaw Lodge has a fine information display and sells teas and coffees, essential after this reasonably strenuous ramble.

Walk 21: Hathersage

The Route: Hathersage, Leadmill Bridge, Hazelford, Stoke Ford, Bretton, Abney, Smelting Hill, Offerton Edge and Hall, Derwent riverside

Distance: 14 km (9 mls)

Start: Hathersage railway station (Grid Reference 232811

Map: Ordnance Survey Outdoor Leisure No 24 – The Peak District; White Peak Area; Pathfinder Sheet 743 – Sheffield

How to get there:

By Train – There is a daily train service from Sheffield and Manchester.

By Bus – There is a daily bus service from Sheffield.

By Car – Travel on the A625 from Sheffield or Chapel on le Frith to Hathersage then on the B6001 (signed to Grindleford) to Hathersage railway station.

The Barrel Inn at Bretton is a very old public house, dramatically situated at almost the narrowest part of Bretton Edge on the former main road from Sheffield to Buxton. The date-stone over the door is 1697, but the landlord and lady believe that there have been inns on the site long before this – possibly since Roman times. It is thought to be the highest pub in the Peak District and, on a clear day, you can see five counties while imbibing a pint or two. The pub, which has two linked rooms and serves hand pulled Bass and Stones is justifiably popular, with seats outdoor for summertime and fires in winter. Bar snacks are available.

The Walk

From the station go to the main road and then turn left under the railway bridge and follow the B6001 road down to the river bridge. There is a footway except under the railway bridge itself. The river bridge spans the Derwent and is known as Leadmill Bridge. The bridge was widened in 1928, having been built in 1709. It replaced an earlier difficult ford, known as Hazelford which carried the packhorse route

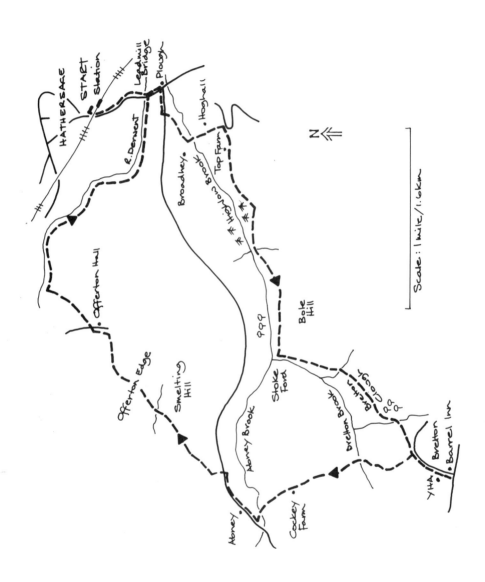

called the Halifax Gate over the Derwent.

At the road junction, just before the Plough Inn, go right, leaving the main road behind and ascend the quiet lane with some fine views of the surrounding valley. After a short distance, the lane bears right and a track continues ahead. Follow the track, which contours around the shoulder of the hill to enter the valley of Highlow Brook.

Hog Hall

The track continues ahead but a footpath sign directs you away from Broadhey Farm down the left through a thorn thicket to a bridge over Highlow Brook. Go over the bridge and follow the path, climbing up a terrace in the hillside. Then follow a field wall past Hog Hall, to a gate and stile which leads into a rough, walled lane. Continue up this lane until it joins another lane at a T-junction. Go right here, following another rough lane towards Tor Farm. Here, the track swings to the right into the farmyard but you go straight on, through a gate into fields again.

Highlow

There follows a very attractive stretch of trackway and on pleasant turf throughout. The route passes through three fields, with lovely views over the Highlow valley to Highlow Hill opposite. The name "low" is derived from the Norse language, "Hlaw" meaning hill. Pass a spring with its stone trough and go through a gate into what used to be Highlow Wood, now felled and re-planted with conifers. Some of the new trees are perilously close to the path and in places the path itself has been churned by forestry activity.

The path descends towards the stream in what can be a muddy scramble but soon bears left, away from the forestry scar to a stile. On the right, a simple plank bridge crosses the main stream alongside a ford – but do not go this way. Instead, cross the tributary stream on the convenient boulder and ascend a worn tractor way up the spur between the two brooks. In spite of the modern tractor ruts this route is ancient, being one of the old packhorse ways in the area. Follow the track as it climbs steadily away from Highlow Brook onto open hillside. The view down the valley from this point is excellent, with Millstone Edge being particularly prominent.

Lonely Thorns

Near two lonely thorn trees the tractor ruts bear left onto the flanks of Bole Hill. This is another well-known place name, indicative of metal smelting – in this case, lead. The metal was smelted in open furnaces known as boles, which relied on natural wind power for the necessary draught, hence their exposed situation on the tops of hills.

Bear right here, and follow the broad green path down towards the river again. As the path descends it enters a little side valley and then an area of scrub woodland. Stoke Ford and its attendant footbridge can be seen below. A narrow path contours left and avoids the final descent. It maintains a level course to first cross the route coming down from Sir William Hill and then joins the path heading up Bretton Clough. Stoke Ford is another convergence point of old packhorse ways.

Bretton Clough

As you walk up Bretton Clough, the path is well defined but narrow. There is one difficult spot where a spring has to be avoided. After that, the path goes over a stile and swings into a deep tributary clough. Without losing much height at all the stream is crossed and a broad green track rises steeply on the far side passing a ruined farmstead. The walked path keeps to open fields here, rather than the route shown on the map, until it enters an area of scrub and meets a very wet section. Most walkers skirt this and pick up the path again as it turns into another deep clough.

Another path joins from the left, and the two descend to a stile. Cross this and negotiate the stream on a stone causeway, whereupon the path makes a bee-line for a curious conical hill, then zig-zags left. This is a classic bit of packhorse route, twisting and turning as it climbs the steep hillside towards Bretton in a worn hollow. The right of way is in the hollow, but obstructed by fallen trees and a new steeper path has been beaten alongside. The path eventually emerges in an open area, from which there is a superb view across the clough to the higher hills beyond.

Follow the route left to a stile. Then, with a wall to your right, climb towards the house, to another stile which leads to a narrow lane. Once this has been negotiated a metalled road is reached. Follow this upwards, passing Bretton Youth Hostel to emerge alongside the Barrel Inn with its breathtaking views.

Retrace your steps down the lane past the youth hostel. Walk down to a house on the left known as "Shangrila" with a cartwheel on the front door. Go left here, the path being signposted along what looks like a private drive. Pass to the right of the house, to a stile which leads into open fields. The path is not distinct and on occasion there might be a bull in this field. Head down the field to a post in the left-hand corner. Walk across the next field with a decent wall on your left down to a stile on the brink of Bretton Clough.

The path now drops steeply, bearing right. It is obvious underfoot. Cross another stile and descend an even steeper slope, eroded badly in places but with steps in other parts. The clough is fascinating to geologists. There are numerous hillocks of shale and grit, formed by landslips. Continue along the path to a clump of silver birch where there is a path to the right, down to a tributary stream. Do not take this route but go straight on, (you can see the path ahead), to reach a footbridge over Bretton Brook. Follow the path, waymarked to Abney, across a stile and another footbridge then climbing steeply up the valley side.

Abney

Where the path levels out there is a stile giving out into fields, in contrast to the wilderness of the clough. Follow the wall on your right to a gate from which Cockey Farm can be seen ahead. Continue to a ladder stile, where a signpost directs you to a track to the right of the farm. Beyond the farm, the track bears sharp left, but the footpath goes straight ahead for Abney which is clearly in view. Head for the ruined building by an electricity line and there is a stile to the right. Negotiate this and go left, as signposted and head across the field to the right of the trees.

Another stile leads to a track which successfully skirts a stream and muddy pool before resuming its bee line for Abney. Abney Clough is away to the right and the track now swings away left to round the edge of the clough. Go right and descend steeply to a fence in which there is a narrow gate (not seen from the track). This leads to an even steeper descent requiring steps in places, to a footbridge over Abney Brook. Across the bridge, the path bears to the left and reaches a stile onto a road. Go right here, through the hamlet of Abney, replete with camping barn and telephone kiosk but no pub or shop. Beyond the last buildings there is a ladder stile on the left by the Abney nameplate sign. Climb over this stile and up a path to another ladder stile, then bear right alongside a wall to a third ladder stile. A fourth quickly follows, but then the path mercifully disgorges onto open moorland.

The narrow path rises gently up onto the moor, giving grand views over Abney and Bretton Cloughs and beyond to the Eastern Edges. At the crossing of paths go straight ahead, still climbing, on to the top of Smelting Hill, another industrial place name.

Continue over the heather moor, noting the piles of stones on the left, which mark the sites of ancient burial mounds known as tumuli. There are extensive views from here to Higger Tor, Carl Wark, Bamford and Derwent Edges and also to Millstone and Frogatt Edges. Just past a broken wall, the evil looking Siney Sitch is crossed by a rudimentary footbridge. Dragon flies, however, like the orange and black pools. Shortly after the stream, a green mound in the purple of the heather on the left marks another tumulus.

Offerton Edge

As Offerton Edge is reached a vista of the Hope and Derwent valleys opens up. The path now descends steeply and imperceptibly joins a well-hollowed packhorse way. This leads across the face of the moor towards Offerton Hall, seen below and ahead. The path changes from one groove to another as dictated by bracken and water. Eventually, near the hall, the path leaves the packhorse track (which caries on to Callow) to bear left down the hillside to a stile, which exits into a lane. This is a local variation to the right of way shown on the map.

Follow the lane down past Offerton Hall, then bear sharp right, still descending, to the lower entrance of the grounds. A gateway on the right leads into open fields and an obvious track bears right across a field to another gate and stile. The track, which has obviously been used for vehicles, crosses the middle of a large field to a stile at the left-hand end of the opposite wall near a prominent ash tree. Cross another stile, here next to a gate and follow the track, down the side of an unkempt hedge, heading straight for the River Derwent. A final spurt between redundant gateposts leads to the river bank path and a signpost. The path continues, to cross the river by stepping stones, which are fine unless the river is in flood. Your way, however, is to turn right at the signpost heading along the well used path on the southerly bank. Look out for kingfishers or the bobbing of a dipper. The riverside path eventually emerges at Leadmill Bridge, where you bear left to retrace your steps to Hathersage railway station.

The Barrell at Bretton

Walk 22: Hope

The Route: Hope, Edale Road, Losehill, Back Tor, Back Tor Bridge, Nether Booth, Rowland Cote, Jaggers Clough, Upper Fulwood, Bagshaw Bridge, Oaker Farm, Townhead

Distance: 14 km (9 mls)

Start: Hope Car Park (Grid Reference 172835)

Map: Ordnance Survey Leisure Series No 1 – The Peak District, Dark Peak Area

How to get there:

By Bus – There is a daily service from Sheffield to Hope which stops at the car park entrance

By Train – There is a daily train service to Hope railway station from Manchester and Sheffield with a 10 minute walk into the village.

By Car – Travel on the A625 road from Sheffield or Chapel-en-le-Frith

---

The Cheshire Cheese is a little out of the village centre along the Edale Road, a pub which makes a point of welcoming ramblers. The pub's name dates back to when "salters" from Cheshire led trains of packhorses and waggons across the Peak District carrying the then-precious salt to Yorkshire. As the economy was still much about bartering in those days, payment for an overnight stay was made in cheese!

The Cheshire Cheese is open all day on Mondays to Saturdays and usual hours on Sundays. Bar snacks are available at lunch and early evenings and there are seats outside. This homely pub with a small bar and a larger room, is well worth a visit – with Stones Bitter and draught Bass drawn by handpump. The landlady says the Cheshire Cheese also has a ghost, but a friendly one.

The Cheshire Cheese

The Walk

From Hope car park, go right and cross the main road. Leave the road, going left along a path by Blacksmiths Cottage. This soon gives out through a kissing gate into fields. Mam Tor can be seen to the left while Losehill rises above the bungalow roofs. The "path" goes through a small housing development, the way out being located as a stile to the left of the school. Walk into fields again and now Win Hill can be seen to the right.

Edale Road

At the crossing of paths, go right, by a caravan to a stile-cum-gate and the Edale Road. Go left here along the road, beside an attractive stretch of river to The Cheshire Cheese. On leaving the pub, continue along the road, under two viaducts which carry the Hope Cement Works branch line across the valley. Just beyond the de restriction signs, go left up a little lane and now begin to climb Losehill. Passing the muddy field,

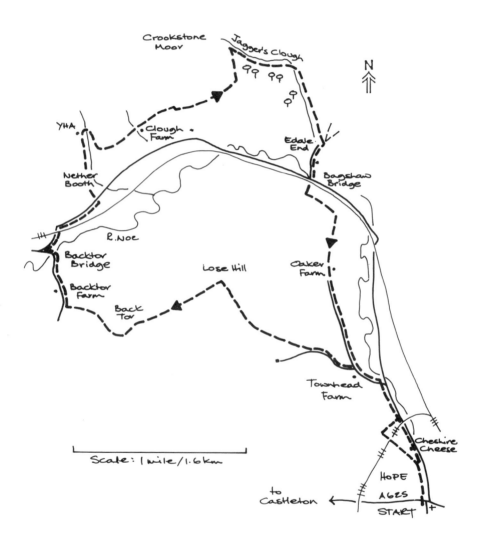

often with horses, on your left, fork left at the junction. Where the lane carries on to Townhead Farm, go right through a stile. It is signed and gives access to an old hollow way and into open fields. A steady climb leads to another stile which is ideal for resting awhile and admiring the view, before ascending what appears to be something akin to a pyramid. Continue up the slope and at the twin stiles and National Trust signs, the path suddenly steepens, so take a deep breath before the final push.

Losehill and Singing Sheep

On the summit of Losehill is a viewfinder and the panorama is quite spectacular. There are tales of singing sheep here – and the authors can vouch for them (before visiting the Cheshire Cheese!). Leave Losehill along the well blazed ridge path soon reaching Back Tor. Take care here for the ridge breaks away into precipitous crags. The main path skirts to the left of the crags by the fence, but the top of Back Tor is worth the visit if you have a head for heights.

Follow the loose and slippery path down by the fence. Be careful here particularly in inclement weather. The path reaches a dip in the ridge. Before the path begins to rise again, go right, to leave the ridge and descend into the Vale of Edale. The path goes over a stile and soon joins a pronounced hollow way which trails in from the right. Back Tor looks spectacular from this angle and the view to Kinder is equally good.

River Noe

At the sign pronouncing the Privacy of the land, go left across a stile in the wall. Continue downwards in the hollow way, with Grindslow Knoll dominating the skyline and Edale Mill, now converted into flats, in the valley ahead. The path reaches a wall and follows it around to the right to a signpost and stile near Backtor Farm. Here, the bridleway from Hollins Cross joins and the two routes continue downwards, skirting the farm, to a stile and gate. Beyond this point, the lane is metalled and descends to Backtor Bridge over the River Noe. It then bears left and ascends to the main road. Here go right.

It is one of the tragedies of the Vale of Edale that there is no decent footpath along the valley bottom. The east-west paths are some way up the hillsides and the north-south paths do not always coincide at the main road. To make matters worse, the road has no footways, so look out for the occasional maniac driver, particularly beneath the railway bridge.

At the approach to Nether Booth, go left up the drive signposted to Edale Youth Hostel (YHA), but the village is a good 2 km away. Edale village is a misnomer. There is no such place! Edale is the valley, and even though the railway station is also called Edale, the village alongside is Grindsbrook Booth, but would anyone guess this?

Cross the cattle grid, noting the monkey flower in the stream on the right. Cross another cattle grid and the drive makes a hairpin bend. Steps lead up onto a terrace in front of the hostel, where another signpost points down to a footbridge across Lady Booth Brook. Once over the footbridge, the path is on the open hillside and there are good views over to Losehill and Mam Tor ridge. The tumbled slopes below Back Tor and Mam Tor show up well. They are remnants of ancient landslips resulting from the weak nature of the interbedded gritstone and shale rocks.

Trekking

The path soon dips to cross another stream at the back of Clough Farm and then performs a similar manoeuvre again shortly afterwards. Ignore paths going down to the farm and stay up on access land. The climb from the second stream is quite steep and the path rises to come alongside a wall. This is followed until, after a stile, the well-worn path slants across the slope to meet a broad bridleway coming up from Clough Farm. You cannot miss this as it is very well used. You are quite likely to meet horse riders along this section as it is one of the favoured trekking circuits.

Follow the track up and over the shoulder and into Jaggers Clough. The place name indicates the importance of this route in earlier times, for a jagger was a packhorse man and this was one of the major Pennine routes. To the left the clough rises to the rocks of Crookstone Moor. Not too long ago, the descent into Jaggers Clough was a messy scramble. The National Trust have now reinstated the old packhorse zig-zag which is far better.

At the stream, leave the bridleway and go straight over the stile signposted to Edale End. Note the mischievous spelling of "style" and see if you can negotiate this one in a dignified manner. The path now enters Backside Wood, a delightful mixed woodland of oak, larch, rowan and full of birdsong. With Jaggers Clough Brook down to the left, the path twists and turns its way through the trees as it descends gradually. Ignore any paths leading off to the right but keep downwards to reach a stile by a footbridge. Cross the bridge and go right, across a marshy area. The path bears away from the stream, climbing a little to a stile. Follow the path alongside the fence to a gate and here go right to join the two paths descending from Hope Cross. A short muddy lane is soon reached.

At the lane go right and then left around Upper Fulwood Farm. This has been finely restored and has a National Trust Information shelter attached, complete with house martins nest. The farm is now the National Trust's High Peak Estate office and workshop.

Bagshaw Bridge

Continue along the lane and over the River Noe again at Bagshaw bridge. Once over the bridge go immediately right and scramble up the bank to a gate at the road. Bearing right, cross the road and go left under the railway into a wet sunken lane. At the end of this (not very far) there is a ladder stile up on the left. Go over this and out into fields again. This is a little-walked path but is clear enough, with a wall to your left.

At the crossing of paths go straight on through a series of stiles and a patch of woodland, until the path becomes confined between two rusty barbed wire fences. On the approach to Oaker Farm the path comes to a gate and a lane. Go right, away from the farm along a now metalled road, past the Countrywide Holiday Association guest house, Underleigh, to rejoin your outward route, where you bear left.

Your outward route can now be retraced, or alternatively, having joined the Edale road, go right at a stile by the letterbox and into fields again. Follow the hedge on the left to a well hidden signpost and stile in the top left of the field and here go left. Pass the bungalow and seek out another stile ahead, to the left of a gate. Another stile takes you out onto a curious concrete suspension bridge over the Hope Cement Works railway line. Beyond the railway, the scant path continues through a series of stiles, passing a brick/concrete inspection chamber to another stile to the left of a white gate.

Pots of Tea

Cross another stile, then head left to a gap in the hedge and a footpath sign to rejoin your outward route near the caravan. Emerge, eventually, opposite the Woodruffe Arms and almost alongside the Woodbine Cafe, where you'll get a grand pot of tea and home-made cakes.

The unusual, solid design of Hope church

Walk 23: Bamford

The Route: Heatherdene Car Park, Yorkshire Bridge, Parkin Clough, Win Hill, Hope Cross, Woodlands valley, Ladybower Dam

Distance: 14 km (9 mls)

Start: Heatherdene Car Park (Grid Reference 203860)

Maps: Ordnance Survey Leisure 1 – The Peak District, Dark Peak Area and Pathfinder Sheet 743, Sheffield

How to get there:

By Bus – There is a daily service to Ladybower from Sheffield

By Train – There is a daily service from Manchester and Sheffield to Bamford then walking via Thornhill and the old railway line to Parkin Clough.

By Car – Travel on the A625 or A57 then onto the A6013, known as Ashopton Road. Heatherdene car park is signposted from the A6013.

The Yorkshire Bridge public house built in 1826, is one of three popular hostelries in Bamford, the others being The Derwent Hotel and The Marquess of Granby. The Yorkshire Bridge is often frequented by ramblers and sells Stones and Tetleys draught beer. It opens from 11 am until 3 pm on Mondays to Saturdays and from 6.30 pm in the evenings. Usual hours on Sundays. Food is served lunchtimes and evenings.

The two large rooms are served by a central bar and in winter both have roaring fires. In summer there are seats outside the inn, offering views across the Derwent Valley to Parkin Clough and Win Hill.

The Walk

From Heatherdene car park cross the A6013 road and go left alongside Ladybower reservoir, with good views across to Ashopton Viaduct and Crook Hill. At the dam there is the fascinating site of the huge overflow weir, like a gigantic plughole. For the most part it is dry but the parched concrete becomes a maelstrom of white water during the wetter winter

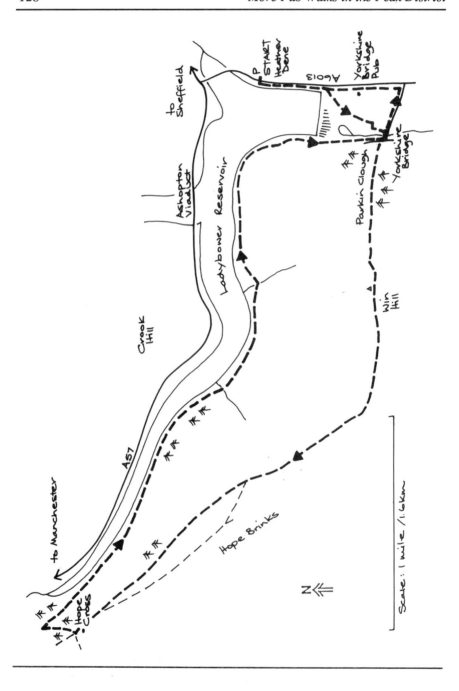

months. On the opposite side of the road is a monument. This commemorates the visit of King George VI and Queen Elizabeth in 1945 when they ceremoniously closed the valves of the dam and began the flooding of the valley. In reality the valves had been closed two years earlier in 1943.

Ladybower Reservoir

The Ladybower reservoir was authorised by an Act of Parliament of 1920. Designed to hold 6300 million gallons of water, the dam is an earth embankment with clay core. The dam itself is 140 feet high at maximum and is 1250 feet long. Work began 15 years later, in 1935, and took 10 years – longer than planned because of the war.

Just before the toilets, go right and follow the path downwards to the "toe" of the dam. Ignore paths deviating left and right, but make sure you pause long enough to read the excellent information board. Continue on the path, bearing left where it joins a track, only leaving this as it approaches the road by a short path to a stile on the right. Bamford

Edge and the Water Board houses clustered around the Yorkshire Bridge pub, are prominent on the left.

At the road, go right and cross the Derwent at the real Yorkshire Bridge. The road swings left, but your way lies to the right along a track leading towards the dam. Almost at once, the way is barred by a gate and stile which is negotiated. Then, a steep and rough path leaves the track and heads away to the left, up into trees.

A short level stretch is soon reached. This was the railway line constructed between 1901 and 1902 for the building of the Howden and Derwent Dams. It was demolished in 1914 when the dams were completed, only to be re opened again between 1934 and 1946 for the building of the Ladybower Dam.

Parkin Clough

Another stile takes you onto an equally steep path beside Parkin Clough. This climbs rapidly through trees to a crossing of paths. Walk straight on here, still upwards among trees to yet another stile. Go right and then immediately left through thinning trees until open hillside is reached and views open up again. Go forward to a twin ladder stile, then up to the trig point on the summit of Win Hill. This is a glorious place on a warm day, but not a place to linger when the wind howls. The view is superb, ranging from Kinder Scout to the west, Bleaklow, Ladybower reservoir and Crook Hill to the north, Derwent and Bamford Edges and the Hope Valley.

The path picks its way through the summit rocks before becoming clear as it heads west. It soon forks at a signpost but keep straight on here, along the broad ridge signposted to Hope Cross. Lose Hill and Mam Tor can be seen ahead, with Castleton to the left. As the path goes through a gap in the wall, the skyline is dominated by Kinder Scout and Crookstone Knoll.

To the right is an experimental moorland regeneration plot, fenced off to prevent sheep grazing, with a considerable contrast in vegetation growth. Keep straight on until the main path veers left, heading down to join the Roman Road from Brough to Glossop. Leave the broad path and follow a narrow path along the ridge top, towards the trees to the right and to a stile in the wall corner. A path then runs between the wall and trees all the way to Hope Cross.

Hope Cross

Hope Cross is not really a cross at all, though there may well have been one here originally. It is a fine example of a guide stone, dated 1737 and carrying the names Sheffield, Edale, Hope and Glossop on its four faces. It may not be in the correct place – the Edale and Sheffield routes cross the Roman Road (from Hope to Glossop) farther west at the next field wall, where the pack horse road, via Jaggers Clough, comes over the ridge.

Door

Leave the cross and go through the door (yes a door) to enter the forest. The pines are gloomy but the path soon emerges into more open woodland before plunging into coniferous plantations again. These woodlands form part of the forest fringing the Derwent reservoirs. The regimented blocks are alien in the Peak District landscape; when felled, let us hope that a more natural form of planting will be adopted. The path soon reaches the ruins of a farm, now almost hidden amid trees, and turns right, following a forest track down to the shore of the reservoir. It can be muddy and has some sections where trees have fallen and not yet been removed.

Ashopton

At the reservoir track go right, enjoying the fine vista over the lake to Crook Hill. Occasional cars may be met loaded up with fishing gear, but otherwise this quiet stretch is a delight. The track keeps to the side of the reservoirs, throughout, rarely deviating from the water and rarely losing sight of it. The viaduct at Ashopton, built in white concrete, shows up clearly but does not look wholly out of place now. Beneath these waters lie the remains of two villages, Derwent and Ashopton, and a number of farms. This was a high price to pay for water supply and at times of very low water the remains can be seen.

The track crosses a bridge and bears left, rising into more woodland which obscures the view of the lake and hides the fact that the route has now turned south. Suddenly, Ladybower Dam comes into view and the track runs alongside the western overflow. There is no access across the dam (though this is likely in the near future), so the track is followed down over the old railway line again. The track bed can be seen disappearing into the dam embankment on the left. Follow the track down to the road at Yorkshire Bridge. In the descent, there's a bird's eye view of the river valley and the outflow from dam.

At the road, go left and walk up the lane to the main road, where you go left to reach the Yorkshire Bridge pub. Buses stop at the pub. The car park is about half a mile farther along, on the right.

The Yorkshire Bridge

Walk 24: *Ashopton*

The Route: Cutthroat Bridge, Ladybower Inn, Ladybower Tor, Whinstone Lee Tor, Hurkling Stones, Highshaw Clough, Moscar House, Cutthroat Bridge. There is an optional extension to Wheel Stones, White Tor and the Salt Cellar

Distance: 7 km (4 mls) or 10 km for the extension (6 mls)

Start: Cutthroat Bridge (Grid Reference 213874

Map: Ordnance Survey Pathfinder sheet 743 Sheffield and Ordnance Survey Outdoor Leisure No 1 The Peak District; Dark Peak Area

How to get there:

By Bus – There is a sparse daily service from Sheffield and Castleton. Alight at Cutthroat Bridge.

By Car – Travel on the A57 from Sheffield or Glossop; there is a lay-by just east of Cutthroat Bridge (Grid Reference 217874)

The Ladybower Inn at Ashopton was originally in the old hamlet which was flooded by the Ladybower dam. Only the pub and a few private dwellings have survived. The pub sign is the Lancaster bomber, a reminder that the Dambusters Squadron (617) practised over the Derwent and Howden dams before their famous raid on the Ruhr dams during the Second World War.

The Ladybower serves Bass and Tetley draught beers as well as food at lunch and early evenings. It is a comfortable pub with one long bar which is needed on high summer days when the pub is very busy.

The Walk

From the bus stop at Cuttroat Bridge walk down the A57 road to go over the bridge which spans the Ladybower Brook. The place gained its macabre name from an incident in 1635. A man was found in Eashaw Clough (now known as Highshaw) with a "wound in his throat" and was carried down to Ladybower House, but to no avail. The present

bridge was not built until 1818, so the dastardly deed must have related
to the old road on which you will soon be walking.

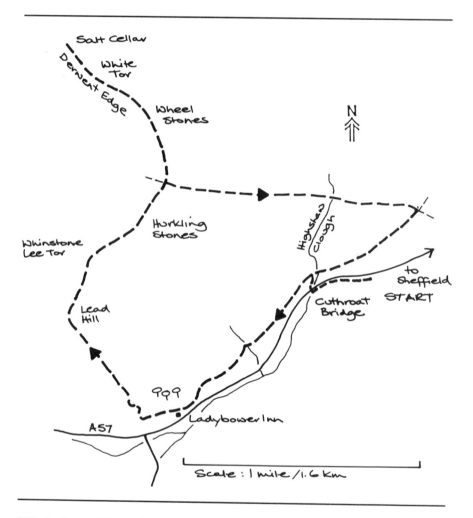

Highshaw Clough

Once over the bridge go right and passing through a gate, turn into
Highshaw Clough. Just before the electricity lines, go left and scramble
up the rocks to a broad path. This is the old road from Sheffield to

Glossop, superseded by Telford's 1818 construction. The old road is a delight to walk on, with good views across to Bamford and Hordron edges, to Win Hill and Ladybower. The road dips to cross a ford, then runs alongside an oak woodland on the left. Shortly, the track forks and here go left, descending towards Ladybower, below the old quarries on the right. The path enters the Derbyshire Wildlife Trust's Ladybower Wood nature reserve. At the gate by the DWT sign the pub can be seen ahead. The path forks. Go left here but remember this spot, as after taking refreshment at the Ladybower public house you have to retrace your steps to this point.

The Ladybower Inn

Viaduct

Having stopped off for refreshment walk back to the spot mentioned above. Then, at the junction go left. The path goes around the rear of the pub and Ladybower House, through Ladybower Wood itself. This is the old road again. As the path emerges from the wood, there is a superb view onto the viaduct which spans the Ladybower arm of the reservoir.

The view of Bamford edge and Win Hill is good. At the corrugated iron gate in the wall on the left, and just by the junction pole, a narrow path leaves the old road and ascends steeply to the right.

At a solitary thorn-bush, the path enters a series of overgrown hollow ways. There is never any doubt about the route, which continues to snake its way upwards to emerge on the summit of Lead Hill. A fork in the path takes the walker left to a cairn which offers a magnificent view of the Derwent valley.

The entire walk along the edge is a delight, with the high moorlands of the Dark Peak dominating the western horizon and the waters of the Derwent dams adding a dash of colour to the scene. From Lead Hill, if the reservoir level is low, the remains of Derwent village can be seen spread out below like a map.

Leaving the cairn, return to the edge path and at the base of the next significant rise there is a crossing of paths. The walk goes straight on here up to Whinstone Lee Tor. For those who are tired, the right-hand path leads unerringly back to Cutthroat Bridge.

Otherwise, continue on the edge path past Hurkling Stones, seen to the right, and then dipping to a signposted cross "roads" with shooting butts off to the right. This is the turning point of the official route and if your are not doing the extension to the walk go right here. However, the Wheel Stones are only 0.5 km ahead and should not be missed. Press on, remembering that you must return to this spot and that the signpost indicates Moscar and Derwent.

The Wheel Stones are well worth a stop and a scramble. Getting to the highest rocks is easy enough. getting off is a different matter. The path runs just to the left of the stones with grand views on all sides. The next pile of rocks is White Tor and this is closely followed by another jumble, shown on the map as Salt Cellar. This is not the name of the group of rocks, but a very apt description of one particular rock. It is shaped very much like an old fashioned salt cellar. It is also easily missed as it lies on the north western side of the pile of rocks, overlooking Derwent reservoir. Only its top can be seen from the path, but if you find that you have reached a wall on your left you've passed the Salt Cellar.

This is a good place to rest before retracing your steps past White Tor and the Wheel Stones to the Moscar – Derwent signpost. Here turn left.

A Landrover track leads off left to the shooting butts but this should be ignored and the narrow footpath followed. It is quite clear through the heather and there are occasional posts to guide. Another line of grouse butts is soon reached, right alongside the route. Then the path, churned up by four wheel drive vehicles, dips to cross Highshaw Clough Brook at what can only be described as a quagmire. Beyond the brook, the track rises and improves somewhat as it reaches the intake wall. Stanage Edge can be seen to the right. Go ahead through the gate and follow the wall down under the electricity line, then right, down to the signpost by two gates.

Old Road

This is an important crossing of paths. Go through the second gate and turn right and you are back on the old Sheffield – Glossop road again. Follow the old road beside the wall to a stile at the far end of the field. This leads onto open moorland again. Ladybower Brook and Cutthroat Bridge can be seen below as the old road keeps company with the power lines to Highshaw Clough.

In spite of the Ordnance Survey map showing the line of the old road across Highshaw Clough as a right of way, it cannot be used. The bridge was demolished in 1818, and there is a 20 foot drop to the brook below. A rough scramble down to the stream is followed by a degree of boulder hopping across the water. A climb up the other side is the only way forward and leads back to the outward section undertaken earlier. Turn left and go through the gate to the newer Cutthroat Bridge and the main road.

Walk 25: Rivelin (Near Sheffield)

The Route: Rivelin Mill Car Park, The Lawns, Moorwood Lane, Ronkesley Hall Farm, Norfolk Arms, Hollow Meadows Brook, Headstone, Brown Edge, Redmires Reservoir, Wyming Brook, Fox Holes Plantation, Allen Sike, Blackbrook, Coppice Wood

Distance: 13 km (8 mls)

Start: Rivelin Mill Car Park (Grid Reference 291873)

Map: Ordnance Survey Pathfinder Sheet 743, Sheffield

How to get there:

By Bus – A good, daily service from various parts of Sheffield

By Car – The car park is signed off the A57 Manchester Road if approaching from the west or Sheffield city centre. Travel on the A6101 Rivelin Valley Road if approaching from the M1 motorway or Sheffield's northern suburbs.

The Norfolk Arms, to be found part way along the walk, is situated on the main A57 road at a place known as Hollow Meadows. The pub's name relates to a time when the Dukes of Norfolk owned substantial tracts of land around Sheffield city. It serves a grand pint of Wards and Darleys on handpulls. The pub is usually open from 11.30 (noon at weekends) until 3 pm and from 7 pm in the evenings. Food is served daily and there is also a beer garden, family room and playhouse (children only, please!). Music lovers might also like to know that there is a trad jazz gathering and a folk club at this thriving pub.

The Walk

Leave the car park by the solitary car access and cross the road to the signboard. This explains the Rivelin Valley Nature Trail and there is a little about past industrial history. All of the mills that were once housed here have gone, but many of the dams remain, havens for wildlife and popular recreation spots for city dwellers.

The Norfolk Arms

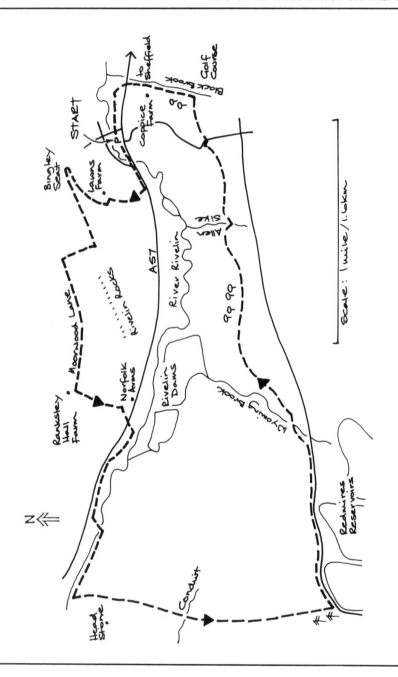

Return to the car park and walk through it onto what is obviously a dam wall. The Rivelin Brook is to the left and a silted mill pond to the right. At the bridge, a fine example of turnpike road architecture, go right along the A57 for a short distance, passing the post office and toilets. Cross the wide mouth of the Rivelin Valley Road with care and then, at the footpath signpost, go right, through a white gate and ascend the track to Lawns Farm.

On entering the farm compound, go left through the yard, past a collection of van bodies, then right, up the hill. The route is shown on the Pathfinder map as a track, but it rapidly deteriorates to a narrow path. This is often muddy and overgrown by nettles and bracken so a stick might come in handy here – and shorts would be sheer masochism. The wall to the right, however, is a sure guide. At the waymark, continue by the wall and mercifully, the path disgorges onto Woodbank Road, which is only a narrow lane.

Bingley Seat

Go left past Bingley Seat and climb the lane, which offers fine views over the valley towards Lodge Moor. The lane climbs steadily, with rock outcropping on the right. Where the lane turns sharp right, the map shows the start of Rivelin Rocks but there is no access to them at this point. Continue along the lane turning left at the T-junction. There's a seat here for those wishing to gaze across the valley and to the moors high above Sheffield.

Moorwood Lane

At the next junction go left and then immediately right, along Moorwood Lane, which is only a cart track. The views up the valley are grand, with Derwent Edge on the skyline. The solitary standing stone on the south side of the valley is the Headstone, which is passed later. The map shows Moorwood Lane going right but this is not obvious on the ground as the cart track continues straight ahead to Ronkesley Hall Farm, a fine Jacobean style building in a commanding position.

At Ronkesley Hall Farm, turn left and go down the hill, with views to Lodge Moor and Rivelin reservoirs. The track soon becomes metalled, swings right as it cuts the line of Rivelin Rocks, then descends to join the

A57. Cross the main road to the footway and go left, down to the Norfolk Arms.

On leaving the pub, retrace your steps to the junction with Ronkesley Lane and continue for a quarter of a mile to The Cabin, a cafe. Here, go left down a track, leaving the A57 behind and soon reach the bridge over Hollow Meadows Brook. There is a choice of routes here with paths either side of the brook. The one on the south side is by far the most adventurous, with parts reminiscent of jungle terrain. The choice is yours, but make sure that you turn right. Both routes eventually end at a small footbridge. If you have chosen the jungle route do not cross the footbridge, but turn left up the path. This climbs rapidly away from the brook and soon leaves the wood behind, emerging onto heather moorland.

Headstone

The views open up again; right to the Wheel Stones on Derwent Edge and left to Lodge Moor Tower. Soon a crossing of paths is reached where there is a guide post. The route of the walk continues straight on, but a diversion to the right to the Headstone is worthwhile for the view. On the main route, continue ahead, following the path up to the conduit. This feeds Redmires reservoirs, catching water from the moors east of Stanage Edge and running for about 3 miles. Cross the conduit bridge and carry on upwards towards a wall corner, then straight on, in the direction of the gate posts rather than to the right. This is the highest point on the walk and the view eastwards is extensive.

Redmires Reservoirs

Beyond the gateway the path is rough, most probably following the remains of an old wall. It dips briefly to cross a muddy stream, then rises again before descending through pine woods to a road alongside Redmires reservoir. Go left here and follow the road down to Wyming Brook, noting on the right the curious inscribed stone in the wall. The inscription reads ISB 1828 and there are three carved fishes.

At Wyming Brook, bear left through the car parking area along a broad track. Almost at once, go right, down the signed path, over a brook on stepping stones, then bearing left and upwards to leave the stream behind. The path is easy to follow, perched on the southern edge of the

Rivelin Valley with fine views interspersed with woodland. The tower of Lodge Moor hospital can be seen to the right.

Allen Sike

The path becomes a track and swings right (ignore the waymark) to dip into Allen Sike. It turns back on itself on the opposite side of the little valley. Where the path forks take the right-hand route which runs slowly up the hill to join Lodge Lane. Throughout this stretch there are grand views of the valley and from Lodge Lane, a particularly good view of the Rivelin Dams.

At Lodge lane, go right, up the hill, then turn left along a signposted path to come to the Maddison Memorial seat, a fine place to sit on a summers day. Check the time with Lodge Moor clock and make your way along the path by the golf course. There's a striking contrast between the wild valley sides and housing seen from here. Where the path forks, go left and down. At the next junction of paths go left again and descend Blackbrook, keeping the stream to your right. The path twists and turns its way through mixed woodland of oak, ash, birch and holly. There are many little side turnings, but the main route is always obvious and the stream a clear guide. Eventually, a stile is reached which leads, a little disconcertingly, onto a well-mown lawn, part of the gardens of Blackbrook Farm (shown as Coppice Farm on the map). Pass considerately across the lawn to a gate and onto the main Manchester Road.

Cross the road with care and descend a bridleway opposite, to the River Rivelin. Ignore paths leading off to the right. Linger by the rapids and pools and cross the bridge, turning left to pass by the Rivelin Valley Nature Trail sign seen at the start of the walk, to reach the car park.

Walk 26: *Little Hayfield*

The Route: Church Mill, Blackshaw Farm, Lantern Pike, Lower Cliff

Distance: 5 km (3 mls)

Start: The Lantern Pike (Grid Reference 034883

Map: Ordnance Survey Outdoor Leisure 1 – The Peak District, Dark Peak Area

How to get there:

By Bus – There is a service Mondays to Saturdays between Glossop and New Mills. A less frequent service runs on Summer Sundays

By Car – Travel on the A624 between Chapel-en-le-Frith and Glossop. There is very limited car parking in the village – so please park considerately.

The Lantern Pike now has one large room broken up with nooks and crannies and a beautifully warm fire on a winter day. It used to be a farm and then became known as The New Inn. A landlady in the 1920s was murdered here and was the subject of national interest when Scotland Yard became involved.

Open at lunchtimes and evenings and serving Tetleys Bitter on handpull from a snug corner bar, this welcoming pub also serves bar meals and has a restaurant area. The interesting pictures and brasses add to the homeliness of the pub. In particular, the framed picture of the *Wayfarer* bus and rail Map: the authors helped launch this 'day rover' promotion over ten years ago!

The Walk

Start the walk from The Lantern Pike by turning right to walk towards Hayfield. Do not turn immediately right by the telephone kiosk, but take the next right turn and follow the lane down to the old Church Mill complex, which has been refurbished as luxury housing. Cross the bridge across the brook just beyond the mill. The path leads up to a stile and then bears left up the bank on stone slabs to join a row of hawthorns. It then bears left up the field to cross another stile near to a house.

The Lantern Pike

Cross Roads

Cut across the drive and head in a similar direction up the hill. Go through a gap and climb up above a wood and cross another stile. Bear right to follow a path alongside a dry stone wall on the right to a walkers' cross roads. Do not trust the directions, however, for the post is often turned by mischievous persons to confuse the unsuspecting rambler.

Lantern Pike

Bear left to walk back across the field, but climbing away to the right. The path is well worn and Lantern Pike (the hill, not the pub) is ahead. Go through the gate onto National Trust land and keep straight on if you'd like to climb up to the monument. Long ago, in times of war and

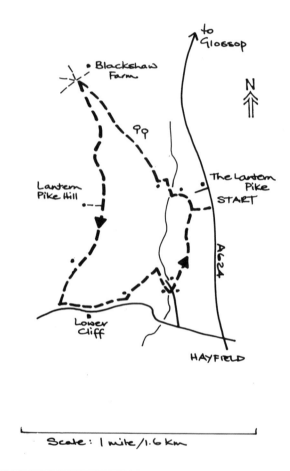

distress, a bonfire would be lit here to spread the message across the land. Such a beacon was lit to warn of the Spanish Armada coming and in recent years this was celebrated with a re-enactment of the event.

Those feeling less energetic should keep to the lower level path which skirts the hill. From the monument or the lower path, make your way to the gate exit in the lower left-hand corner. The view across to Hayfield and beyond is illuminating. You can see how it is in a basin and why mills developed with the flow of the streams.

Birch Vale

The path joins a track and continues down the hill to a tarmac road above the Sett Valley. Bear left and walk along this until the road bends right and dips more sharply by a row of solid houses. Keep ahead here to pass by the houses and go through the gate on to a bridleway. This soon comes to a junction. Turn right here and drop down to a very pleasant setting of Birch Vale House by the old mill complex. Having crossed the bridge walk along the drive for twenty paces or so before cutting off left through a gate into a field.

Walk along by a small dry stone wall, then climb away from the buildings, up the field and along a well worn path to a stile. Cross this and proceed ahead between a wall and fence. This becomes a track leading to Slack Lane. Go right to the main road and retrace your steps to The Lantern Pike.

Clough Mill, nestling beneath the shoulders of Lantern Pike

Walk 27: Alport

The Route: Snake Inn, Dinas Sitch Tor, Oyster Clough, Cowms Moor, Hayridge Farm, Alport Bridge, Blackley Hey, Blackley Clough, Crookstone Knoll, Madwomans Stones, Blackden Edge, Blackden Rind, Seal Stones, Gate Side Clough, Fairbrook Bottom

Distance: 15 km (9 mls)

Start: Alport Bridge (Grid Reference 142895). Limited Parking only

Map: Ordnance Survey Leisure – No 1 The Peak District – Dark Peak Area

How to get there:

By Bus – There is a Summer Sunday service only from Sheffield and Manchester

By Car – Travel on the A57 from Sheffield or Manchester. Alport Bridge is not signed, so be vigilant or you will miss it.

The Snake Pass Inn stands on one of the last great turnpike roads to be built across the Pennines in the 1820s, following a successful petition to Parliament by the Duke of Devonshire and other worthies. The road linked Glossop to Sheffield, but the stretch to the old Ashop Inn, now submerged beneath the Ladybower reservoir, proved too much for the horses. A staging post was needed and the then Lady Clough House was built with a toll bar. 'Snake' derives from the badge of the old Cavendish family (the Dukes of Devonshire) – the original crest was unfortunately removed in the early 1920s. The land now used for car parking was known as "The Little Meadow" and during the last century many a famous prize fight took place here.

The Snake Pass Inn is open from 10.00 am in the summer and throughout the day. Winter opening is from 11 until 3pm and from 6pm in the evening. Draught beers are served from Bass, Tetleys, Theakstons and Websters and a wide range of bar snacks at lunchtimes and early evenings. Walkers are very welcome at this inn as there is a Hikers' bar open during summer. There is ample room for families, but the publicans ask customers to remember the points made in the introductory chapter.

Those interested in ghostly happenings might like to know that there is a resident ghost in the old stables, thought to have been a labourer from Ladybower reservoir who took his own life. He's a kindly ghost so do not worry!

The Snake Pass Inn

Warning

This is not a walk to be undertaken lightly. It traverses the northern scarp of Kinder Scout, the highest part of the Peak District. Although there is a path all the way, in parts it is narrow and could easily be lost in mist. If the weather is inclement, or there is a mist over the tops, do not venture on this one unless competent with a compass and map. The descent to the Snake Pass is rough and so stout footwear is essential. Having said all this, it is a challenging and invigorating walk which brings out the thirst in best tradition.

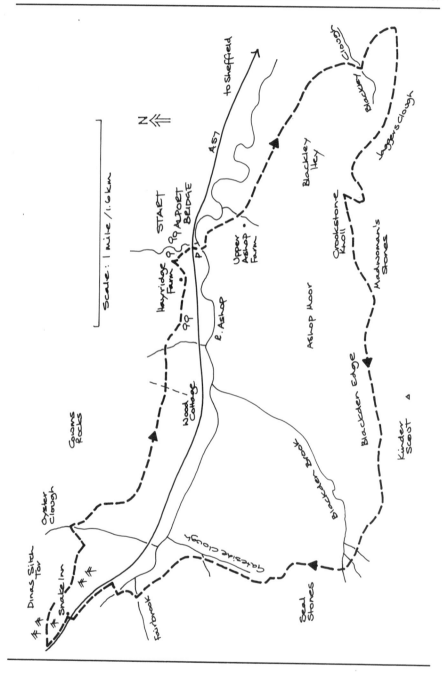

Scale: 1 mile / 1.6 km

N

to Sheffield

A57

START
ALPORT BRIDGE

Hayridge Farm

Upper Ashop Farm

R. Ashop

Wood Cottage

Gooms Rocks

Oyster Clough

Dinas Sitch Tor

Snake Inn

Fairbrook

Blackden Brook

Gateside Clough

Seal Stones

Ashop Moor

Blackden Edge

Kinder Scout

Madwoman's Stones

Crookstone Knoll

Blackley Hey

Blackley Clough

Jaggers Clough

River Ashop

From the car parking area at Alport Bridge, descend the track to the River Ashop and either ford the river if it is low or use the footbridge a short distance upstream. The incongruous concrete weir and equipment are part of the Derwent dams complex, water being taken out of the Ashop here and fed into the upper reservoirs. The course of the aqueduct can be seen snaking down the valley but there is no right of way there.

Climb the track up towards to Upper Ashop Farm, bearing left as the farm is approached and dipping to cross a small stream. A gate gives out into open country. This is access land and there is a right to roam here, but it can be very hard going. Your way is to follow the track, bearing right where it forks and gently ascending the flanks of Blackley Hey. This is the route of the Roman Road from Glossop to Brough and a fine walk it is too. As height is gained, the view of the Ashop valley becomes better and better, stretching to Derwent Edge, Stanage and Bamford Edges, the twin topped Crook Hill and Win Hill. Just as the track dips into Blackley Clough, Crookstone Knoll can be seen to the right.

Best Route

The best route is to continue along the track for a short way to a gate. Imperceptibly, you have topped the pass from the Ashop and are now heading in the direction of the Hope and Edale valleys. Do not go through the gate, but turn sharp right by the "Boundary of the Open Country" sign and join a narrow path leading up the hill at roughly 45 degrees to the wall. The path climbs steadily to join a broader track by two wind-battered and stunted trees. The formidable Crookstone Knoll is now in full view ahead.

Follow the track to a stile and gate, then come out onto open moorland. The path narrows abruptly and winds its way through tussocky grass and peat. It climbs steadily, bearing to the left of Crookstone Knoll and giving good views into the deepening 'V' of Jaggers Clough.

Crookstone Knoll

A short stony scramble takes the path onto the top of a small crag. Here the path splits. take the right-hand route which skirts another small rocky outcrop and arrives on the plateau of Crookstone Out Moor where the edge path is met. Go right, along the edge path to Crookstone Knoll top and savour the magnificent panorama.

At Crookstone Knoll, the edge path turns sharp left. You cannot miss this as to do so would entail dropping off the very steep northern end of the knoll. Head in a westerly direction along the edge path, keeping steep ground to the right. There is a view right up the Snake Pass from here. The path forks after about 400 metres.

The edge path proper is the right-hand one, which descends slightly to a shooting butt before rounding the end of an unnamed spur. The walk, however, takes the left fork towards rocks on the skyline. At the rocks go right and head across the moor to another jumble of rocks known as Madwomans Stones. Pick up the path again beyond the stones as it makes a beeline for another little rocky outcrop and trig point at 590 metres. Keep the rock outcrop to your left. The path tends to the right, crossing a deep grough before descending to rejoin the edge path again at Blackden Edge. If your navigation is correct you should be looking across the Ashop Valley and the Snake Road, straight up Oyster Clough to Bleaklow. If you have Mam Tor and Lose Hill in your sights, you have gone astray and no doubt the authors will be cursed!

Blackden Brook

Go left along the edge path to the impressive cleft formed by Blackden Brook. The path winds its way across steep slopes through rock outcrops and piles of stones to cross a series of little brooks, often dry in summer, before reaching Blackden Brook itself. Cross the brook and continue along the edge path which picks its way through the rock maze and turns northward. After about 400 metres, the path swings left again to continue in a westerly course. The Snake Inn can be seen below. As you swing left and your eye is drawn down to the Snake Inn, you should see a path running down by the side of a wall and stream before disappearing into the nick of a steep-sided clough. This is Gate Side Clough and is the key to a successful descent.

Seal Stones

Keep walking west for about 250 metres on the edge path. The stones scattered all around on the moor are known as the Seal Stones, though the resemblance seems minimal. On your right and just below is a line of rocks and a narrow path leaves the edge path and descends, steeply and roughly to the right of these. Once at their base, the wall leading down to Gate Side Clough can be seen and the "path" descends even more steeply and roughly to meet it. The wall is followed down to a point just short of the entrance to the clough, where the path does a quick left shuffle through a gap, crosses the stream and turns right to follow the brook down. This bit is usually wet and at one point the path fords a tributary stream where the rocks are slippery.

Once beyond this point the path improves markedly as it enters Gate Side Clough. The clough is very deep and plunges steeply down to the Ashop, but the path stays high on the clough side, descending gently before heading down to the end of Fairbrook. This path was built for access to shooting cabins and butts and was able to take horses and carts, so it is well constructed.

As it nears the bottom of the slope the continuation path bears left into Fairbrook Bottom to avoid sheep pens below. At Fairbrook, the path drops down a shaly, slippery slope to the river which is forded as best you can. Go right on a broad track round to the bridge over the Ashop. Despite the thousands of walkers who pass this way, the path beyond the bridge, through the woods to the stile on the A57 is by no means clear. However, the roar of the traffic is a sure guide and as the road is neared the path becomes clearer again. At the road, go left to the Snake Inn but take care as there is no pavement here.

Dinas Sitch

On leaving the pub turn right, up the road, crossing with care. After a short distance, the path up the Ashop valley goes off to the left. Opposite, a signed concessionary path climbs up through the forest. Cross the road and go up this path until it joins another track below the conifer shrouded Dinas Sitch Tor. This is a most unusual place name for these parts for it is Welsh meaning "stronghold".

The right of way soon emerges into open fields. The path is waymarked across the field with pegs and seems at odds with that shown on the map. The path comes close to the edge of the woods again. It suddenly widens and appears to be paved, but this is only the fragments of a broken wall. The track is constrained between the hillside on the left and trees on the right. Where it opens out, do not descend alongside the trees nor go left along a prominent track on the left. Instead, take the middle course, a narrow, scarcely visible path down to the wall and then to Oyster Clough.

Cross the stream and cross a stile, following a wall on the right to a gate and stile leading into open fields again. The path is again waymarked with pegs, past a circular sheepfold to a stile. In the next field there are traces of genuine paving. This is likely to belong to the packhorse era rather than Roman, but is a reminder nevertheless of the former importance of the route before the A57 was built.

Cowms Rocks

The path now runs alongside a wall through a convulsed landscape at the foot of Cowms Rocks. This is evidence of landslip brought about by the fragmentary nature of shales and grits in this area. A ladder stile leads from this zone. Across the valley ahead you can see the Roman road you climbed at the start of the walk.

Cross the track leading down to Wood Cottage and continue along an obvious path which soon dips to cross a stream. There is evidence of alternative routes here, shown as grass-covered grooves. Beyond the stream and ladder stile the path keeps on the left-hand side of a deep hollow way, the opposite side of which has lengths of revetment walling to hold back the loose sides. The path then swings into a deep wooded clough and here is more evidence of alternative routes including the remains of bridge abutments. Continue over another ladder stile and down a hollow way, but before reaching Hayridge Farm, bear left across a field to a stile in the corner. Go into the next field, where a narrow, barely distinguishable path, leads across it to join a lane to the left of the fence corner. There is a good view of the great landslip of Alport Castles ahead.

At this fence corner go right, over a stile and descend towards the River Alport crossing another ladder stile into a little wood. Go over another stile to regain the A57 at Alport Bridge opposite the car parking spot. Public transport users should keep an eye on the time on this walk as the Summer Sunday service is none too frequent. The walk is demanding but the climbs and views reward the efforts.

Ashop Valley

Walk 28: Dungworth

The Route: Dungworth, Hill Top, Bents Farm, Load Brook, Beeton Farm, Rod Moor Road, Crawshaw Lodge, Crawshaw Farm, Royds Clough, Corker Walls, Hall Broom, Ringwood Lane, Dungworth

Distance: 9 km (6 mls)

Start: Royal Hotel, Dungworth (there is on street parking just to the south of the pub) (Grid Reference 279897)

Map: Ordnance Survey Pathfinder Series 743 Sheffield

How to get there:

By Bus – There is a service from Sheffield but it is irregular and infrequent

By Car – The journey provides an interesting technical exercise in map reading. Travel on the B6077 from Malin Bridge (North West of Sheffield) to Damflask, then follow the signs to Dungworth.

The grandly named Royal Hotel at Dungworth is the only pub in the village and is a classic local. The pub sells Websters Yorkshire Bitter and John Smiths on hand pull and sells nuts, crisps etc. Walkers are allowed to consume their own food at lunchtimes. The Royal is open from noon until 3 pm Mondays to Saturdays and from 7.30 pm in the evening. Usual Sunday houre. This is a welcoming hostelry with an open fire in the bar during winter time. Just the setting for the locals to sing carols on Sunday lunchtimes in the months leading up to Christmas.

There is a very impressive view across to the all-year ski run and outside there is a picnic table bordering Yews Lane. Altogether, a good local with a welcome for visitors.

The Walk

On leaving the pub, turn left along the road then left again at the junction with Sykehouse Lane. Go up Cliffe Hill for a short way then go right, over a stile into open fields. The path is signposted from the road.

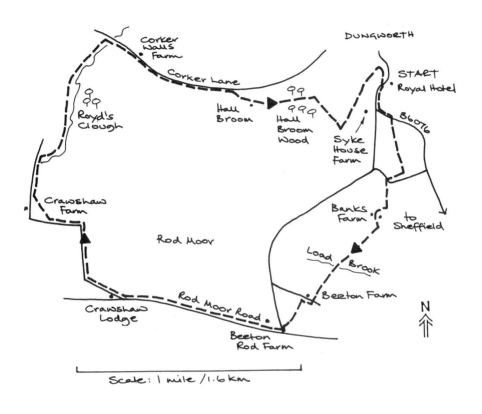

Scale: 1 mile / 1.6 km

Continue up the fields, keeping close company with the wall on the left until George House Farm is reached. Look out for puff balls in the fields as the farm is approached.

The path is signposted around to the left of the farm buildings over a tree trunk stile. The path emerges on the farm lane and follows either branch of this down to the road. Go right here, along the road until it bends sharply to the right. At this point go left down a signposted footpath between two gardens to reach a stile and open fields again. Keep left here, by the wall to a stile, then continue ahead as shown by a waymark to another stile which disgorges into a narrow lane. This is not as shown on the map, but is evidently a recent official diversion.

Load Brook

Go right, up the lane which passes through the middle of Bents Farm. Notice the curious barn on the left. At the T-junction just beyond the farm go left down a walled track by the side of the farm house. This track is Bents Lane which descends to Load Brook. However, at the point where there are three gates, go right, over the stile alongside the wall. The path follows a well defined tractor way through a gate and then across the next field to finish abruptly in a patch of gorse. Diligent searching will reveal a narrow path through the gorse and a well-hidden stile in the wall.

Go over this and walk diagonally across the next field to the Load Brook. It is tempting to follow the stream up the valley but this is not the way. There is a decrepit stile, passable only by those with Olympic aspirations on the opposite side of the stream by the hollybush. A path leads from the stile, up beside the wall to another wall ahead. The way, which is not obvious on the ground, is sometimes interrupted by low-level electric fencing here when there are cattle grazing.

The access track to Beeton Farm crosses the route. Go right here, through the gateway and into the farmyard. In the yard, go left then right by the barn to another gateway. Immediately beyond this gate leave the farm road and go over a stile on the left. Then, follow the wall up towards the road. Again, the path is not distinct but as you approach the road there is a little bridge made out of railway sleepers over the ditch. This is followed by a stile and then Beeton Green Road is reached. Go left and then right at the cross roads. There's a good view over Sheffield from this point and on a clear day you can see the cooling towers of Ferrybridge power station, many miles away to the north east.

Walk along Rod Moor Road, past Beeton Rod Farm with its gateposts made of old concrete rollers. On the left, the view is down to Rivelin Valley with Lodge Moor and the Headstone on the far side. Ahead, the hills of the central Peak show up in the Moscar gap, where the A57 road begins its descent to the Derwent Dams.

At Crawshaw Lodge (about 1 km from the crossroads) bear right up the drive, which is a public right of way. The track skirts the buildings, passes through a gate and stile and comes out onto open moorland. Still climbing the track swings abruptly right and a grand view opens up ahead. The eye is drawn through the Moscar gap, with Stanage Edge on the left, Derwent Edge and the Wheel Stones on the right, to rest on Win Hill, Mam Tor and the great bulk of Fairbrook Naze. Keep on the track until it turns sharp left to descend to Crawshaw Farm, seen below. Where the track reaches the wall corner a stile on the right accesses a field and thus avoids the farm buildings. The path through the field is not obvious. Make a beeline for the right-hand end of the new building, diagonally across the field and reach a stile by a gateway. On crossing the field avoid piles of stones in the ground, as there is a disused shaft shown on the OS map!

Royds Clough

The path emerges onto the farm road again. Here, go right, down the concrete track to cross Royds Clough stream in a culvert by the wood. The track runs to a gateway but there is a waymarked gate stile on the right leading into the wood. Go through this and follow the wall on your left until it kinks left. Now make your way ahead and down to pick up a distinct path on a terrace.

The path descends easily through the trees of Royds Clough, with the stream below. There are one or two wet patches, especially in the lower part of the clough where the terrace ceases and the stream bank is followed. Eventually, a wall across the route forces the path up and left, away from the stream. Follow the wall which soon kinks to the right and is reinforced by a wire fence. A recently fallen tree partly blocks the path and means a small deviation into the wood. Be vigilant, for there is a ladder stile just beyond the tree and it is easily missed.

Go over the ladder stile with care as some of the rungs are rotten. An indistinct path then crosses the field towards the stream again, finally reaching it at a metal gate which surprisingly is waymarked. Go through the gate and then keep alongside the fence by the stream. Pass a farm bridge to reach a stile which drops you into Corker Lane by a short flight of steps. Go right and across the road bridge, not forgetting to look over to see the attractive little waterfall. The road rises away from the stream and shortly passes Corker Walls Farm, a substantial place built in 1838, with few apparent concessions to modernity.

Corker Lane

Continue along Corker Lane ignoring the signed track to the right. There are good views down to Damflask reservoir from here. As the road begins to descend again, about 3 to 400 metres beyond the track, look out for a well hidden footpath sign on the right. An equally well hidden stile takes you over the wall and into a steeply sloping wilderness of bracken and scrub. There is no obvious path, but the easiest passage seems to be alongside the wall to the right. Eventually the "path" joins a track leading to Hall Broom. Skirt around Hall Broom and follow the track down to the old mine workings where the lane swings left. Go through the stile on the right and continue ahead (ignoring the sign and stile on the right) with the wall on your right until Hall Broom Wood is reached. The path then negotiates the remnants of a stile on the right and enters the wood. There is a view here across to Bradfield, The Rochers and beyond to White Tor on Derwent Edge.

Damflask reservoir

Sheffield

The path climbs easily up through the wood to a stile. Go right here alongside the wall and as you breast the rise Sheffield comes into view. A couple of stiles are crossed before reaching Ringwood Lane, but it seems no longer to be a lane, as there is only one wall with the scant remnants of a hedge to mark the other boundary. Go left here and the lane soon becomes walled. Where the track goes off right to Syke House Farm, continue ahead through the stile by a gate along a walled lane, here little more than a narrow path. The pub is now tantalisingly in view to the right, so a quick sprint is required along the remainder of Ringwood Lane to the road. Go right to reach the pub, which stands just beyond the Ebenezer Methodist church a veritable thirst after righteousness!

The Royal Hotel, Dungworth

Walk 29: Tintwistle

The Route: Holybank quarry, Stonebreak quarry, Valehouse reservoir, Bottoms reservoir, Tintwistle bridge

Distance: 6 km (4 mls)

Start: Old Oak public house (Grid Reference 019973)

Map: Ordnance Survey Outdoor Leisure No 1 – The Peak District, Dark Peak Area

How to get there:

By Bus – There is a regular bus from Manchester and Glossop

By Car – The A57 then A628 from the West and the A628 from Sheffield direction. There is limited on street parking off the main road.

The Old Oak is a small terrace pub featured in the Good Beer Guide selling Tetley Bitter on draught. Local legend has it that Dick Turpin took cover in the village and possibly supped at the local inns. As Dick spent most of his career down south this is hard to believe. There were, however, dozens of highwaymen of a similar ilk and no doubt the sighting could have been one of his brethren who specialised in robbing people travelling by coach through the Woodhead Pass.

The Old Oak does not usually serve food. It is open from noon until 4 pm and from 7 pm in the evenings on Mondays to Thursday; all day Friday and Saturday. Usual Sunday hours prevail. Also in the village is the Bulls Head serving Bass beers.

The Walk

Turn left from The Royal Oak and then shortly left again off the main road onto Old Road. Pass The Bulls Head, a war memorial and a small green and then the houses huddled around Higher Square and Lower Square. Follow the road around by a methodist chapel, allowing a view over Padfield and beyond. Before the next cottage, go left up a green lane towards the old Holybank quarry, by heather-laden banks as indicated by a yellow marker.

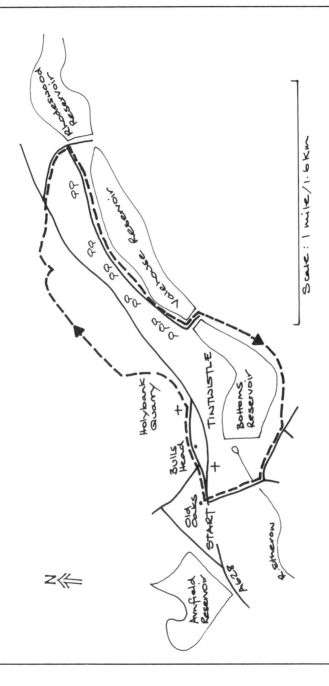

Open Moorland

The path leads to the edge of Tintwistle and out onto open access land. At the first crossing of paths at the start of the old quarry working cut back right along a narrow path to a signpost indicating "Open Countryside". Proceed to the ladder stile ahead and cross it. The easiest route is to simply turn right afterwards and follow the wall. For those who wish to gain ground and a good view up the valley, walk ahead through the old spoil heaps.

Do not go too far, however. Aim to bear right along a path which descends across the moorland towards the wall again, a path which is no more than a sheep walk. This rises a little, then falls to run parallel to the wall. The path bears right down a steeper bank to join another curving wall seen below on the right.

Valehouse Reservoir

Join a bridleway (blue waymarks) which in turn comes to a main track. Go right to the main A57 road. Cross the road and turn left but within a matter of a few metres go right, down the access road to the reservoirs. Before the dam, turn right through gates to join a concessionary path alongside Valehouse reservoir, which uses a road where a railway was once laid to build the dams. This runs between the very pleasant Valehouse Wood and the reservoir.

Wildfowl

In winter the reservoir attracts a variety of wildfowl. The road reaches the dam of Bottoms reservoir. Turn left here to cross the dam and then right at the other end as waymarked with a yellow marker. This well-used path follows a field line above the reservoir, through stiles (but ignore the one on the left leading away towards Hadfield and the ladder stile down to the reservoir on the right). Instead, continue ahead as the path climbs away above a small tree belt to a group of houses. The path exits onto the Padfield main road and bears right to pass down the one way street, Goddard Lane, to an old public water fountain dating from 1879. This was erected by the Manchester Corporation Waterworks. It needs to be restored.

Turn right to follow the road over the River Etherow. Then go up the bank to the main road in Tintwistle for the pub or bus.

Walk 30: Langsett

Route: Langsett Car Park, Langsett Village, Langsett Dam, Upper Midhope, North America, Hingcliff Common, Crookland Wood, Langsett

Distance: 5 km (3 mls)

Start: Langsett Car Park ((Grid Reference 210005)

Maps: Unfortunately, this walk requires three maps Ordnance Survey Outdoor Leisure No 1, The Peak District Dark Peak Area, Pathfinder No 726 Sheffield and Stocksbridge, and Pathfinder No. 715 Barnsley

How To Get There

By Bus – There are daily services from Sheffield, Barnsley and Manchester

By Car – From the West, travel on the A57/A628 to Flouch then A616. The car park is signposted just before Langsett. From the east Travel on the A616 from the M1 to Langsett, where the car park is found just beyond the village. Take care when driving into or out of this car park as the A616 is a very fast road.

The Waggon and Horses, a CAMRA Good Beer Guide entry for years, is a classic coaching inn. It sits gable end to the main road but with the main entrance onto the old village street. This pleasant two-room pub, often with a real fire in the bar during the winter months, serves a choice of real ales Theakstons, Bass and Youngers on handpull and rather good homemade baking. There is a beer garden but unfortunately, the roar of the A616 detracts from its tranquillity.

The Walk – to North America and back

Go towards the entrance of the car park but, instead of going onto the main road, seek out a path in the right hand corner. There is a well hidden signpost. The path briefly runs parallel to the main road then turns right up a ginnel to emerge in the old part of the village near the reservoir house. The pub lies just to the left.

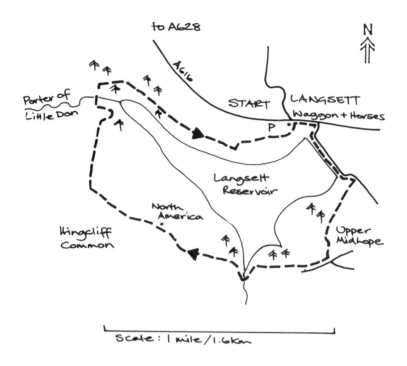

On leaving the pub, go to the main road and turn right onto the footway and after a short but horrid stretch with lorries moving far too fast, turn right again at the road junction signposted to Strines and Derwent Valley. Follow the road around and onto the dam. Langsett Reservoir was built between 1896 and 1904 for Sheffield Waterworks. The reservoir first overflowed in January 1906. For those who enjoy such historical detail by far the best companion is Bowtell's book "Reservoir Railways of Manchester and The Peak ".

From the dam there is a grand view down the valley towards Stocksbridge. Follow the road as it bends first left then right (no footway), then go right at the bridleway sign at the end of the trees. The bridleway runs alongside the trees, gradually rising with increasing views down the valley.

Upper Midhope

As the bridleway approaches the metropolis of Upper Midhope, the way forks. Follow the yellow waymark to the right. The route continues along an old lane, once surfaced but now very overgrown. It emerges in Upper Midhope and goes left between the solidly built farm buildings. Look out for the water works sign and bear right here between buildings and down a grassy lane to join a metalled road near the hairpin bend. Go right here along a private road, but still a public footpath, though concreted. Where the track forks, go straight on into the woods on the fringe of Langsett reservoir. Like so many reservoir plantations conifers dominate, but they soon thin as the track dips to come alongside a small inlet of reservoir where the Thickwoods Brook flows in. The brook is spanned by a substantial bridge, giving a glimpse back across the reservoir to Langsett. The track then rises again, away from the lakeside, with the moors to the left and the ubiquitous conifers to the right, known by the unusual name, Mauk Royd.

North America

Eventually the track forks. Ignore the left hand path but carry along the right hand track, which climbs steadily onto the moor soon revealing the white tip of Emley Moor TV mast over the top of trees on the right. At the "Boundary of Open Country" sign, you reach North America. The sad remains of this former farmhouse look out on the reservoir which finally destroyed it. The farm overlooked a pit at Rushy Lea where clay was extracted and taken to build the core of the dam.

Little Don

Go through the ruins onto a clear track with remnants of slab paving and climb onto Hingcliff Common where the Cut Gate track is reached. Two forlorn gateposts mark the spot. This is an ancient packhorse way from the Derwent valley over to Penistone and is a superb walk but not the route for today. Turn right and descend towards the western extremity of Langsett reservoir and the valley of the Porter or Little Don river. This is a very attractive section, with wide views over the moors into the valley and the full length of the reservoir. Both Emley Moor and Holme Moss masts can be seen. Unfortunately, the course of the A628 over Fiddlers Flat is all too obviously marked by the procession of lorries.

Mystery Railway

Where the track meets a wall, the path bears right, descending alongside the trees in a large zig-zag. The direct path has been stopped off to counter erosion. The track swings right to cross a rather fine stone bridge, but sharp eyed rail historians will spot the remains of railway sleepers embedded in the ground and to the left a few lengths of narrow gauge rail. It might well be a remnant of the railway system used to build the dam, but the rail looks more modern and is something of a mystery.

Cross the bridge and go steeply up the hill, passing a rocky outcrop on the left. Look out for a narrow path to the right leading into the wood (not signposted). Take this path through the wood, eventually coming alongside a wall which fringes the reservoir. On a clear, sunny day the view of the water and the encircling trees is delightful, with an abundance of birdlife too.

The lakeside path is eventualy forced to go sharp left and climb steeply through the trees, assisted in places by steps to a little gate high above the water. This brings you out of the wood onto another path by a disused quarry. The quarry was the source of stone used to build the dam and the path you are now on was the old railway line to it. Go right and soon you reach the back of Langsett car park.

Sample the delights of country pubs, and enjoy some of the finest walks with our expanding range of 'real ale' books:

PUB WALKS IN THE PEAK DISTRICT
– Les Lumsdon and Martin Smith

PUB WALKS IN LANCASHIRE – Neil Coates

PUB WALKS IN THE PENNINES
– Les Lumsdon and Colin Speakman

PUB WALKS IN THE LAKE DISTRICT – Neil Coates

PUB WALKS IN THE YORKSHIRE DALES – Clive Price

PUB WALKS IN THE COTSWOLDS – Laurence Main

PUB WALKS IN OXFORDSHIRE – Laurence Main

HEREFORDSHIRE WALKS – REAL ALE AND CIDER
COUNTRY
– Les Lumsdon

PUB WALKS IN CHESHIRE – Jen Darling

– all 'Pub Walks' books are just £6.95 each

There are even more books for outdoor people in our catalogue, including:

EAST CHESHIRE WALKS – Graham Beech

WEST CHESHIRE WALKS – Jen Darling

WEST PENNINE WALKS – Mike Cresswell

NEWARK AND SHERWOOD RAMBLES – Malcolm McKenzie

RAMBLES AROUND MANCHESTER – Mike Cresswell

WESTERN LAKELAND RAMBLES – Gordon Brown

WELSH WALKS: Dolgellau and the Cambrian Coast
– Laurence Main

OFF-BEAT CYCLING IN THE PEAK DISTRICT – Clive Smith

THE GREATER MANCHESTER BOUNDARY WALK –
Graham Phythian

THE THIRLMERE WAY – Tim Cappelli

THE MARCHES WAY – Les Lumsdon

– all £5.95 except where indicated

We also publish:

Guidebooks for local towns

A guide to the pubs of 'Old Lancashire'

Spooky stories

Myths and Legends

Football books

and, under our Sigma Press banner, over 100 computer books!

All of our books are available from your local bookshop.

In case of difficulty, or to obtain our complete catalogue, please contact:

**Sigma Leisure,
1 South Oak Lane,
Wilmslow, Cheshire SK9 6AR**

Phone: 0625 - 531035 Fax: 0625 - 536800

ACCESS and VISA orders welcome – call our friendly sales staff or use our 24 hour Answerphone service!

Most orders are despatched on the day we receive your order – you could be enjoying our walks in just a couple of days.

An Invitation

Sigma Leisure is expanding and always on the lookout for new books, and of course, new authors to write them!

Our current range includes:

❏ An extensive range of rambling books

❏ Our very popular range of "Pub Walks"

❏ Town & Village guides to the North West

❏ Local history and folklore

❏ Activity interests including Mountain Biking and Football

Future publications include:

❏ Advanced Driving

❏ 'Days Out' for families with small children

❏ Authentic pubs

We plan to develop into other leisure areas very soon, with a focus on sport, entertainment, keep fit and personal health.

Our speed of production and successful marketing could make a great success of your book. So if you are interested, and have an idea for a book for the leisure market, then why not telephone us on *(0625) 531035* for further information or alternatively, write to us at our office:

Sigma Leisure,
1 South Oak Lane, Wilmslow, Cheshire, SK9 6AR
Fax: (0625) 536800